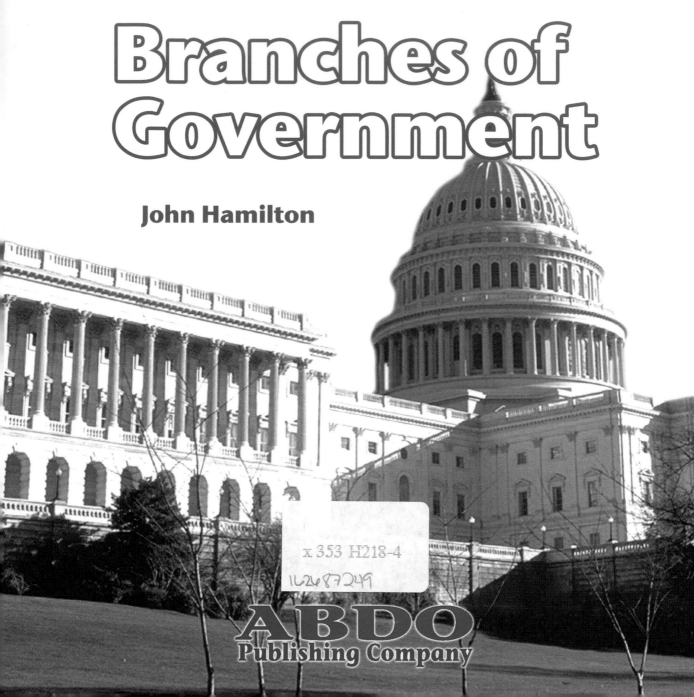

Branches of Government

John Hamilton

ABDO
Publishing Company

visit us at
www.abdopub.com

Published by ABDO Publishing Company, 4940 Viking Drive, Edina, Minnesota 55435.
Copyright © 2005 by Abdo Consulting Group, Inc. International copyrights reserved in all
countries. No part of this book may be reproduced in any form without written permission from
the publisher. The Checkerboard Library™ is a trademark and logo of ABDO Publishing
Company.

Printed in the United States.

Cover Photos: Corbis
Interior Photos: AP/Wide World p. 15; Corbis pp. 1, 5, 6, 7, 8, 10, 11, 12, 13, 14, 18, 19, 20, 21,
    27, 29, 31; Getty Images pp. 9, 17, 20, 22, 23, 24-25, 26

Series Coordinator: Kristin Van Cleaf
Editors: Heidi M. Dahmes, Kristin Van Cleaf
Art Direction & Maps: Neil Klinepier

Library of Congress Cataloging-in-Publication Data

Hamilton, John, 1959-
    Branches of government / John Hamilton.
        p. cm. -- (Government in action!)
    Includes index.
    ISBN 1-59197-644-8
    1. United States--Politics and government--Juvenile literature. [1. United States--Politics
and government.] I. Title. II. Government in action! (ABDO Publishing Company)

JK40.H36 2004
320.473--dc22

                                                                              2003063877

Contents

For the People

People often talk about the government. "The government passed a new law." Or, "Government leaders met today to discuss important foreign issues." But what is a government? Why is it necessary?

A government is an organization that oversees affairs for a group. It creates and enforces laws and provides services. People create governments to protect societies, as well as individuals. They are an important part of human life and history.

Governments have existed in many forms. People have had many ideas on how to best support their society. There have been experiments with government forms such as monarchy, totalitarianism (toh-ta-luh-TEHR-ee-uh-nih-zuhm), and democracy.

One of the first large-scale experiments with democracy was in the United States. The country's **Constitution** created a representative government with three branches. Over 200 years, it has grown into a working democratic government that is still successful today.

*Tourists view the U.S. Constitution at the
National Archives Building in Washington, D.C.*

Ways to Govern

People have had many theories on how governments should be run. As a result, governments come in many forms. Countries around the world have experimented with different ideas for hundreds of years.

For example, monarchy has been a common form of government throughout history. In a monarchy, a king or queen governs. Many monarchs believed that God had chosen them to rule. A monarch rules for life and then hands the title down to his or her oldest child.

Faisal I was king of Iraq from 1921 to 1933.

Benito Mussolini (left) *and Adolf Hitler were totalitarian dictators during World War II.*

A dictatorship is run by a single ruler who holds all the government's power. A dictator usually rules through force and deception. This person keeps power by demanding obedience from the people and by using violence.

Similar to a dictatorship is totalitarianism. This type of government is controlled by a small group of people from a single political party. It has control over every part of the people's lives. The state is considered the most important part of life. So, the people have few individual freedoms.

Government theories can even promote no government. In anarchism, people believe there should be no official government or laws. They think these things suppress the people. Instead of government, citizens would work and live in self-governing groups.

Democracy is another type of government. The word means "rule by the people." In this system, the people have the final say in how their government is run. As a result, citizens can limit their government's power.

A man exercises his right to vote in 1994 during the Republic of South Africa's first free election.

In a democracy, all citizens have the same individual rights. These rights are protected by a government that the people control. Citizens exercise control by voting in free elections. The majority makes the final decision.

Democracy is practiced in different ways. In a direct democracy, the people make all decisions. Everyone votes on every issue. This works best in small groups. A representative, or indirect, democracy is more practical in larger communities such as countries.

In an indirect system, people elect fellow citizens to represent them. The representatives make laws and vote on issues on behalf of their **constituents**. This is a republic. The U.S. government is an example of a representative democracy and a republic.

An East Timorese woman supports indirect democracy by voting in an election for the government assembly in 2001.

The United States

General George Washington and the Continental Army

The United States began as 13 colonies. They were controlled by England and its monarch. Then from 1775 to 1783, the colonists fought for their independence in the **Revolutionary War**. They created their own government and founded the United States.

This first government was established by the Articles of **Confederation**. It gave the states a lot of individual power. However, problems arose when the states could not work together. The central government did not have the power to keep control.

In 1787, the **Founding Fathers** met in Philadelphia. They knew the country needed a stronger central government. However, they did not want it to have the power to take control away from the people. In the end, they created the U.S. **Constitution** and the **Bill of Rights**.

The U.S. Constitution was approved in 1788. It is the world's oldest written constitution that is still in effect.

The **Constitution** is still the supreme law of the land. It **guarantees** the equality and individual rights of the people. In the United States, citizens who are 18 or older elect a president and representatives to government positions. So, the government is run by and for the citizens.

In the United States, each state has its own government. They share power with the central government. This is called federalism. This design was laid out by the Constitution.

The states create their own governments. But the Constitution maps out the central, or federal, government. It divides the federal government into three branches. They are the legislative, executive, and judicial branches.

This division of the government into separate branches is called separation of powers. The **Founding Fathers** did this in order to keep the central government from gaining too much power. Each branch has its own duties, which are separate from the other two.

The Massachusetts House of Representatives meets in this chamber in Boston.

Alabama's capitol is in Montgomery. It was built in 1851 and is the state's fifth capitol building.

Legislative Branch

The legislative branch of the U.S. government was created by Article I of the **Constitution**. This branch is a bicameral legislature. This means it is divided into two parts with equal power. They are the House of Representatives and the Senate.

Together, the House and the Senate are called Congress. Members of Congress meet in Washington, D.C. Their main job is to write and pass laws.

The House of Representatives has 435 members. The number of representatives in each state is determined by the state's population. Members serve two-year terms. The entire House is up for election every even-numbered year.

Both chambers of Congress meet in the Capitol, in Washington, D.C.

Members of the House of Representatives are sworn in on January 7, 2003.

Members of the House select a Speaker of the House to lead. The Speaker sends proposed laws to committee discussions and assigns people to special committees. He or she also schedules **debates** and votes in the case of a tie.

The Senate is smaller than the House. It is made up of 100 senators, which is two from each state. Senators are elected for six-year terms. Every two years, about one-third of the Senate's seats come up for election.

The vice president of the United States serves as president of the Senate. He or she votes in senatorial **debates** if there is a tie. When the vice president is absent, the Senate chooses a president pro tempore (proh-TEHM-puh-ree), or "president for a time."

In both houses, the political parties each choose a majority leader and a minority leader. These leaders arrange schedules and plan the lawmaking **strategies** of their parties. The parties also choose assistants called whips.

Congress considers thousands of laws every year. When a law is being debated in Congress, it is called a bill. A bill can begin in the House of Representatives or in the Senate.

After a bill is introduced, it goes to a committee. There are committees for each of the major subjects with which Congress deals. In committee, the members discuss changes and prepare the bill to be voted on.

Then, the bill goes back to the House or the Senate, where the lawmakers vote. If approved by one house, it goes on to the other house for another vote. If the second house approves the bill, it is sent to the president. If the president approves, he or she signs the bill into law.

Senator Joseph Biden speaks at a Senate Foreign Relations Committee hearing.

Executive Branch

The executive branch was created by Article II of the **Constitution**. Its duty is to carry out the laws created by the legislature. This branch is made up of the office of the president and a number of departments and **agencies**.

The president is in charge of the executive branch. He or she is often called the chief executive officer. This position is elected every four years through a system called the Electoral College. The president may only serve two terms.

The chief executive officer has several duties, such as dealing with laws. He or she suggests laws and develops programs to solve national issues. The president also reviews bills passed by Congress.

Ronald Reagan (left) *stands with his wife, Nancy, as he is sworn in as the fortieth U.S. president in 1981.*

The president's Oval Office in the White House

The Electoral College

The U.S. president is chosen in an indirect election. Instead of electing the president, voters actually choose electors to represent them. Each state has the same number of electors as it has members in the U.S. Congress. Together, the electors are called the Electoral College.

The Electoral College meets in December to cast votes for president and vice president. The electors usually base their votes on how the people of their home states voted. In January, Congress counts the votes. The candidate with more than half of the electoral votes wins.

The executive branch also enforces laws. This is done through 15 departments. The heads of the departments are appointed by the president and make up the cabinet. These people give the president advice. In addition, many

President George W. Bush meets with his cabinet members.

independent **agencies** create rules and programs for the nation.

Another duty of the president is to serve as commander in chief of the U.S. armed forces. The president appoints chief military officers. He or she also decides how large the military will be.

President George H.W. Bush and Soviet leader Mikhail Gorbachev sign a treaty in 1990.

In addition, the president directs the country's dealings with other nations. He or she makes treaties and appoints ambassadors. The president also

suggests laws dealing with international affairs. The secretary of state advises him or her in this area.

The vice president works with the president. This person takes over if the president cannot do his or her job. If the chief executive resigns or dies, the vice president becomes president.

The vice president also attends meetings of the president's cabinet. He or she is a member of the Domestic Council, which recommends policies to the president. In addition, the vice president serves on the National Security Council.

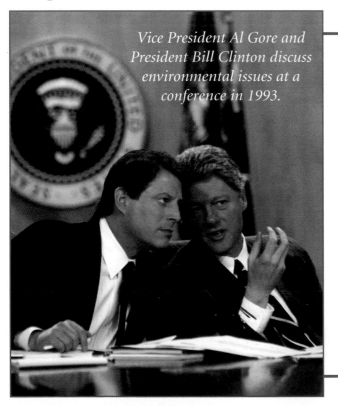

Vice President Al Gore and President Bill Clinton discuss environmental issues at a conference in 1993.

Nine vice presidents have taken over as president due to the death or resignation of the president.

- *John Tyler*
- *Millard Fillmore*
- *Andrew Johnson*
- *Chester A. Arthur*
- *Theodore Roosevelt*
- *Calvin Coolidge*
- *Harry S. Truman*
- *Lyndon B. Johnson*
- *Gerald R. Ford*

Judicial Branch

Above the stone columns in front of the U.S. Supreme Court Building are the words Equal Justice Under Law.

The third government power is the judicial branch. Its duty is to review how laws are used. To do this, Article III of the **Constitution** created the U.S. Supreme Court. It also granted Congress the power to create other courts.

The federal courts settle disputes involving federal laws or the Constitution. They also hear cases between citizens and the federal government. The federal courts may decide cases between individuals or groups from different states. And, they hear cases involving other countries.

The Supreme Court is the nation's highest court. It has the final word on whether a law is **constitutional**. The Court is made up of nine justices. One chief justice leads eight associate justices.

In 1789, Congress passed the Judiciary Act. This established the lower federal court system. It includes trial courts, which are known as federal district courts. The United States has 94 district courts, with at least one in each state. There are also courts in U.S. territories such as Guam.

Supreme Court Justice Anthony Kennedy stands in his chambers in the Supreme Court Building.

The federal court system also has appellate courts. If a case is challenged, one of these courts will review the decision made by the district court. There are 12 appellate courts and one Court of Appeals for the Federal Circuit. Each represents an area called a circuit.

The judicial branch also includes two special courts. The Court of International Trade deals with cases involving international trade and **customs** issues. The Court of Federal Claims settles cases against the federal government.

There are also courts that are technically a part of the executive branch. They include the U.S. Tax Court, the U.S. Court of Military Appeals, and the U.S. Court of Appeals for Veterans Claims. Although these courts are part of the executive branch, appeals of their decisions can be taken to the judicial appellate courts.

Many district courts do not allow cameras in the courtroom. Instead, artists make sketches of the trials.

Checks & Balances

The U.S. government is set up so that there is a separation of powers. Related to this is the system of checks and balances. This system helps keep the government from abusing its powers. And, it keeps one branch from becoming too powerful.

Each branch has a check on the other branches. For example, the executive branch can **veto** bills passed by Congress. To balance the judicial branch, the president nominates the U.S. attorney general, Supreme Court justices, federal court judges, and U.S. district judges.

Bill Clinton vetos a tax bill in September 1999.

A newspaper headline announces that the Supreme Court has ruled segregation in schools unconstitutional.

In the legislative branch, a two-thirds majority can pass laws over a president's **veto**. The Senate must approve a president's Supreme Court nominees. Congress can also change the number and **jurisdiction** of federal courts. And, Congress must also approve any decision to go to war.

The judicial branch uses judicial review to check the legislative process. This means that the Supreme Court can declare a law **unconstitutional**. This is the most important power held by the judicial branch. It prevents the other two branches from becoming too powerful or **corrupt**.

By the People

    Governments exist to serve and protect their citizens. To do this, governments pass laws and make sure these laws are enforced. They promote justice through the court system. Governments organize armies to defend their nations. Some even encourage education and **cultural** unity.

    The U.S. government is based on the idea that people have certain rights. The **Founding Fathers** believed that the reason to have government is to protect these freedoms. This is why they wrote the **Constitution** and the **Bill of Rights**.

    These documents spell out the powers of the U.S. government. But this government has its limits. In order to protect people's rights, checks and balances limit how much control the government branches can have. In America, the ultimate power in government lies with its people.

    The United States has lasted over 200 years because of its citizens. Americans support their government by actively participating in it. They vote to keep a government they approve of in power. It is truly a government by the people.

Children show their support for their country in an Independence Day parade.

Glossary

agency - an administrative section of a government.

Bill of Rights - a summary of rights in the U.S. Constitution that the United States guarantees to the American people.

Confederation - a group united for support or common action.

constituent - someone who allows another person to represent him or her.

Constitution - the laws that govern the United States.

corrupt - to change from honest to dishonest in morals or actions.

culture - the customs, arts, and tools of a nation or people at a certain time.

customs - taxes or fees charged on imports or exports by a country's government.

debate - to discuss a question or topic, often publicly.

Founding Fathers - the men who attended the Constitutional Convention in Philadelphia in 1787. They helped write the U.S. Constitution.

guarantee - to make sure or certain.

jurisdiction - an area where a particular group has the power to govern or enforce laws.

Revolutionary War - from 1775 to 1783. A war for independence between Britain and its North American colonies. The colonists won and created the United States of America.

strategy - a plan of action.

unconstitutional - something that goes against the laws of a constitution.

veto - the right of one member of a decision-making group to stop an action by the group.

Web Sites

To learn more about the branches of government, visit ABDO Publishing Company on the World Wide Web at **www.abdopub.com**. Web sites about the U.S. government are featured on our Book Links page. These links are routinely monitored and updated to provide the most current information available.

Index

THE MYSTERY WATERS
OF TONBRIDGE WELLS

The
MYSTERY WATERS
of
TONBRIDGE
WELLS

by Teri Martini

ILLUSTRATED BY LINDA BOEHM

THE WESTMINSTER PRESS
PHILADELPHIA

PUBLISHED BY THE WESTMINSTER PRESS ®
PHILADELPHIA, PENNSYLVANIA

PRINTED IN THE UNITED STATES OF AMERICA

Library of Congress Cataloging in Publication Data

Martini, Teri.
   The mystery waters of Tonbridge Wells.

SUMMARY: When seven persons vanish in the eerie mists of an English meadow, twelve-year-old Laura and her clairvoyant friend Elliot piece together a number of strange facts and incidents to solve the mystery.
   [1. Mystery and detective stories]   I. Boehm, Linda, ill.   II. Title.
PZ7.M3672Myu   [Fic]   74-28313
ISBN 0-664-32565-3

Contents

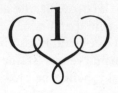

The Mystery Waters

Ever afterward, Laura remembered that summer as the summer of the Nailbourne. Early in June there was a drought.

"We be in for evil times if it don't rain soon," said Giles, the gardener's boy, in a mournful tone.

"Yes," said Laura sadly. "The flowers will die, I suppose."

She loved the gardens that surrounded Covington Castle and spent as much time in them as her mother and governess would allow.

"Aye, the flowers will die," said Giles, "but it were not them I be thinkin' of. It be the evil waters of the Nailbourne I mean. The drought brings them on, so I've heard."

The way Giles spoke surprised Laura. He truly sounded frightened. Of what, she did not know, then, and dismissed it all as foolish superstition. When Giles was called away, she wandered back to the terrace.

From the position of the sun, Laura determined that it

must be teatime. She stopped a moment beneath the terrace and stood idly admiring the beauty of her father's gardens. In spite of the drought, the grass was still green, though there were thin patches. The graceful, winding paths were lined with colorful blossoms, and in the center fountain stood the marvelous statue of Pan, his head raised to the clear sky, while he blew soundlessly on his pipes. How often she had wished the statue alive, a companion for her in this lonely garden.

Gradually Laura became aware of voices above her. Lady Simpson-Favorite had come to call. She and Mother were having tea on the terrace. From where Laura stood, she could not be seen, but she could hear every word.

"Well, he is definitely coming!"

Lady Simpson-Favorite's voice was distinctive. It was deep and full. If she sang, she would be a contralto, thought Laura and prepared to leave. She was not adverse to listening and she often did, but she usually found adult conversation boring at best. Her mother's next comment, however, gave her pause.

"Oh, my dear! Your nerves will never stand the strain of an eleven-year-old boy. You're not in the least used to children. They can be quite a trial, always needing attention and getting sick at unfortunate moments," Lady Caroline Covington told her friend.

A boy nearly her own age coming to live at the Simpson-Favorites'! Laura was delighted. She lived in a house of females. There was Mother and Miss Haversmith, her governess, as well as Laura's older sister, Alexandra. There was Father, of course, but he was home so seldom that Laura had learned not to depend upon him for male companionship.

Boys seldom came to visit Covington Castle. Those who

had, intrigued Laura. They seemed so much more amusing than girls. Now here was a boy come to live right nearby. Why, they might see each other every day. Play together too.

"I daresay you are right, my dear," said Lady Simpson-Favorite.

She was well on in years, much older than Laura's mother, and her voice seemed now to tremble a bit.

"But you see, it is my duty. Elliot was my only true nephew. Now that he is gone, there is no one to care for the boy. The mother died quite mad, you know. We can't expect help from her side of the family. No, I shall have to take him in."

Lady Simpson-Favorite sounded resigned to her difficult fate. She had never married and was used to her solitude.

Mad! The boy's mother had been mad. A little thrill of excitement made Laura tremble. Would the boy be mad too? She could not wait to find out. She ran to tell the others.

Miss Haversmith was presiding over tea in the nursery. Laura was not overly fond of her governess. She was a small, severe woman who pulled her dark hair straight back from her bony face. Seldom had Miss Haversmith smiled upon Laura. Alexandra was her pet.

When Laura burst into the nursery, Miss Haversmith set down her teacup and covered her face with both hands.

"Not a step closer, young miss. Not one step until you have washed and changed your pinafore. When will you learn to behave like a lady?"

Laura knew her dark curls were in disarray, and she looked down ruefully at her soiled white clothing. That had happened when she was helping Giles in the garden.

9

They had been transplanting tulips. In her excitement Laura had forgotten about the dark soil that had fallen onto her clothes.

Miss Haversmith had warned Laura again and again not to associate with the gardener's boy, but Laura ignored this advice. Actually Giles was not much fun. He was so old, past fifteen. But she enjoyed the gardening, and Giles was someone to talk to.

Now she hurried to her room and was back in a matter of minutes, anxious for some of the chocolate cakes she had seen on the silver tray and bursting with her news.

Alas, the cakes were gone when she returned!

"There's to be a new boy at the manor," Laura announced, consoling herself with the fact that she did have news. She was gratified to find that neither Alexandra nor Miss Haversmith knew about the boy.

"A boy?" asked Alexandra, turning her serene gaze upon Laura.

Alexandra was rather lovely, and she knew it. Her long red hair, like Mama's, was smooth and shining, and she had a perfect oval face.

"What boy?"

Laura sipped her tea complacently and finished a cucumber sandwich before she told what she knew. She enjoyed having everyone's attention. It was so seldom hers.

Alexandra sniffed when Laura finished her story.

"I do hope we shan't be expected to entertain him. Boys of that age are so rough and noisy."

Alexandra could hardly have thought otherwise. She was thirteen and nearly a lady. She would have very little in common with boys.

"I hope he never, ever comes to call," she added.

"A boy whose mother was mad!" cried Miss Haversmith. Her dark brows shot up in sheer horror. "It is not likely that your father would think him a suitable companion."

But Miss Haversmith was wrong. Only a week later they were all, even Father, having tea with Elliot Simpson-Favorite and his great-aunt.

Sir Edward Covington welcomed Elliot warmly.

"I had not seen your father in many, many years, but we were boyhood friends. I was most fond of him. I hope you will look upon our home as yours and visit often."

Elliot thanked Father solemnly and then fell silent. Laura watched him eagerly. She liked the way he looked, although she wished he would smile. Elliot had dark hair and eyes that were very nearly black. He was small-boned, not much bigger than Laura herself. If he were mad, he did not show it.

Lady Simpson-Favorite was already exhibiting signs of strain. She held her lavender scarf to her forehead.

"Oh, Sir Edward, you are more than kind. I hardly know where to begin with Elliot."

Laura thought her father was handsome. He was tall and had deep-blue, intelligent eyes. He stood now beside Mother's chair and bowed to Lady Simpson-Favorite.

"Not at all, Lady Madelaine. Not at all. My daughters will be happy to make the boy feel at home. Perhaps he should like to see the gardens."

Elliot seemed uncomfortable to hear himself talked about as though he were not there. He appeared to be even more distressed when Alexandra begged to be excused.

"I find I have a most dreadful headache," she said.

So it was that Elliot and Laura found themselves alone.

"You don't have to show me about. I'm used to being

on my own," said Elliot, as they moved away from the terraces.

"But I want to," said Laura so fervently that Elliot believed her and he smiled.

"How jolly to have a proper garden and so many trees to climb! We had nothing, not even a small garden in London. Do you ever climb?" he asked.

"Oh," cried Laura. "I have always wanted to climb the trees, high into the topmost branches. I should think it would be lovely, like being part of the tree and the sky. But with no one about to show me how to get started, I'm afraid I've been too timid. The branches all look so far above the ground. How does one begin? Perhaps now—" She broke off and gazed hopefully at Elliot.

"Of course," agreed Elliot. "We shall climb together."

He glanced back at the terrace where the adults were still chatting. "But perhaps not today." He gave her a conspiratorial wink.

Laura laughed. "Of course. Not today, but someday."

How delightful Elliot had turned out to be and not in the least mad! Laura led him along the winding paths in and out of the openings among the yew hedges that separated the various gardens. Elliot admired everything.

"The only garden we ever had was in India when I was very young. I hardly remember it at all. Mother and I spent many hours in that garden. It was she who encouraged me to climb into the trees. Once she even showed me herself." Elliot smiled at the memory.

Laura was amazed. A grown woman climbing trees! Perhaps it was part of the madness. She thought it best to change the subject.

"How wonderful to have lived in India! You must tell me all about it."

"It was a strange land, a mysterious land. One can only begin to guess at the mysteries there. I lost my mother in India, you know. She died when I was nine years old." Elliot's eyes clouded.

"I am so sorry," said Laura.

Elliot sighed. "I suppose I'm used to it now. I don't think about her all the time as I did for a while."

"Yes, that's best," said Laura.

They came to the last garden where an apple tree grew in the far corner. They could see its pale-pink blossoms waving above the stone wall. They could hear voices too.

"Look there, I tell you! There!" It was Giles who spoke, and he sounded both excited and fearful.

As Laura and Elliot stepped through the rounded archway, they saw Giles and one of the gardeners standing on the opposite wall, their backs to the children.

"Lord! Lord!" said the gardener in an awed voice. "The Nailbourne! It's come again. God help us all!"

With complete disregard for her station as a lady, Laura rushed forward and scrambled up the wall, finding footholds in the rough stone. Elliot was right beside her. He reached the top first and helped her up.

They stood beside Giles and followed his terrified gaze. There, in what had only yesterday been a dry riverbed winding lazily through the meadow, was now a narrow stream that appeared to be growing fuller and deeper each moment.

"Where did it come from?" asked Laura in astonishment. "It was never there before, and it hasn't rained in two weeks. What does it mean?"

"It's the Nailbourne," said Giles. "Didn't I say it? The evil times has come."

Laura turned to Elliot to see what he was making of all

this. But Elliot was staring past her at Giles. He seemed hypnotized, and there was a look of complete horror on his face. At last he turned and jumped to the ground. Laura hastily followed him.

"What's wrong?" she cried, running to keep up with his swift strides.

Elliot's expression had not changed. He shook his head sadly.

"Poor devil! Poor, poor fellow!" he murmured.

It was all he would say.

Laura was frightened. Was this madness?

Lost in the Mists

Laura and Elliot had nearly reached one of the garden houses before Elliot's rapid pace began to slacken. He had bolted like some wild, frightened creature. What could possibly have upset him so? As they approached the little house, Elliot turned to her.

"I say, could we rest here a moment?"

"By all means," replied Laura.

She was glad he had suggested it himself. It would not do for Elliot to return to the terrace in his present condition. His face was so flushed, and he was still breathing rapidly. For a moment there he had been simply terrified. And yet there had been nothing to frighten anyone. Just Giles and the other man. They were harmless. Of course, there had been the Nailbourne. But that was more mysterious than frightening. It certainly could not account for Elliot's behavior.

The white marble garden house was a small replica of a Grecian temple. Elliot and Laura went in and sat down on one of the stone benches. The little house was domed and without walls. Long, graceful columns encircled it.

Gnarled limbs, bearing white and lavender wisteria blossoms, clung to the stone and perfumed the air.

Laura sat very quietly and watched Elliot, who stared into the distance with unseeing eyes. She did not speak for fear of disturbing him. At last he turned to her.

"What exactly is a Nailbourne?"

Laura was a little surprised by the question. She had been expecting something else, an explanation perhaps. She thought Elliot might want to confide in her. But no, he was only curious about the mysterious stream.

"I don't know," said Laura. "Giles mentioned it only this morning. I believe he called it 'evil waters.' It does seem curious that waters should simply appear so mysteriously. I do know that only yesterday that stream bed was dry. But how water could be evil, I cannot imagine. Why would Giles say such a thing, do you think?"

"Ah," said Elliot softly. "Evil waters! I daresay. I daresay."

Laura did not consider that an answer to her question. Elliot seemed to be talking to himself. Did he think the waters were evil? Is that what had frightened him? Madness or not, Laura was determined to know the answer.

"Elliot, whatever made you say what you did about Giles?"

Elliot turned his dark eyes to hers. They were as opaque as black stones in the sunlight. For a moment Laura thought he was angry. Perhaps she had done the wrong thing. After all, it might be part of the madness. For some reason, she had the impression that those who were mad were also secretive.

Elliot did not seem disturbed by her question. He only seemed puzzled.

"Say? How do you mean?" he asked. "What did I say?"

"Why, you called Giles a poor devil. I wondered what you could mean by that. Why is Giles a poor devil?"

"A poor devil!" Elliot shook his head. "Did I say that? I didn't mean to. Please, take no notice of it. Sometimes I speak without thinking. It's a dreadful habit, I know. Tell me," he said quickly, as though he wanted to change the subject, "do you ride? Aunt Madelaine has given me a wonderful horse. I'd like to go riding, but it would be so much more fun to have company, and I don't know my way about yet."

Laura was bewildered. She had seen the look of horror on Elliot's face. She had not imagined it. Elliot had called Giles a poor devil. Then he had rushed off as though a devil were chasing him, and now he wanted Laura to forget all about it. She did not think she could. But she did manage to pretend. After all, Elliot was her guest. She hesitated only a moment before answering politely.

"I love to ride. We ride every morning before breakfast—Alexandra, Miss Haversmith, and I. When Father is home, he joins us. Would you care to come along? We should be glad to have you with us tomorrow."

Elliot smiled happily. He seemed completely recovered from his fright.

"I say, that would be splendid."

Laura was glad to have cheered him, though she did think he might have been more open with her. What was he hiding? He was a strange boy, but she liked him. It would be pleasant to have him go riding with them. They could show him the countryside. It would be like exploring.

Miss Haversmith, however, was not at all pleased at the

prospect. After the Simpson-Favorites returned to the manor, she voiced her feelings to Alexandra, making certain that Laura heard every word.

"It is one thing to be polite and entirely another to come under the spell of madness. It was hardly necessary to invite that boy to go riding," she said. Disapproval made her sharp features even more severe.

"I quite agree," said Alexandra.

Laura said nothing. She did not agree. Elliot might be a little odd, but she did not think him mad. Except for that brief moment on the wall, he had behaved quite normally. She did not plan to deny herself Elliot's friendship for the sake of that one moment.

Because Father was home, Alexandra and Laura dined with their parents, far from Miss Haversmith's grim warnings of the dangers association with Elliot was bound to produce. It was very pleasant.

After dinner they sat together for a time in the drawing room. Father told them about London and the people he had seen on his last trip. Laura loved listening to Father talk. He had the most marvelous stories to tell, and he did the funniest imitation of the very portly Duke of Paddington, hobbling into the House of Lords on a cane with his big, gouty foot all wrapped up in miles of bandages.

They all laughed, only Mother tried not to.

"Edward, it is really unkind. The poor man!"

But she laughed again just the same.

Laura thought her mother looked especially pretty that evening. Her blue eyes were bright, and her fair cheeks flushed with excitement. All because Father is home, thought Laura.

"Oh, Father, couldn't you stay with us always? Must you be away so much?" she asked.

18

Sir Edward sighed and stroked his daughter's curls affectionately.

"These are difficult times, my dear. Difficult times! No one knows what the French are planning to do next. Some men actually talk of invasion. And then there is trouble on the seas. The French try to board our ships and steal both men and cargo."

"It's always the French," said Mother sadly.

"Not always, my dear." Father's voice was gentle. "These are difficult times, and we must all make sacrifices, but soon things will be different. We must look forward to happy, peaceful days."

He twirled one of Laura's curls about his finger.

"And you, my dear, can't be too lonesome now that Elliot's come. I'm glad you like him. I hope, Laura, that you'll be good friends. I'm so pleased you asked him to ride with us tomorrow. I am looking forward to it."

Laura was looking forward to the ride as well. Perhaps Father was right. If she and Elliot did become good friends, perhaps she would not miss her father quite so much.

Laura went to sleep thinking pleasant thoughts, completely unaware of the fear that gripped the village. By morning all of Tonbridge Wells was in an uproar because of the appearance of the Nailbourne. In the night, fear swept from cottage to cottage and at last reached Covington Castle.

Laura was awakened by low voices just outside her door. She yawned and stretched lazily. The sun was just coming up. Today would be lovely, especially because it would begin with a ride in the company of Father and Elliot. Gradually, however, the voices outside her door became more distinct.

"Parker's own brother was taken the last time, twelve years ago."

That was Mrs. Worthington, the housekeeper. She was talking about Parker's brother. Parker was the butler. Laura had heard that Parker's brother had died under mysterious circumstances long ago. Why was Mrs. Worthington talking of him now? Sleepily, Laura raised herself to her elbows.

"They say Parker's brother was walking across the meadows toward the cove when it happened," Mrs. Worthington was saying. "The mists just swelled up suddenly, surrounded him, and when they were gone, so was he. Disappeared! No one ever saw him again. Oh, Martha, let me tell you. No man is safe when the Nailbourne appears. Not even the master. Not even Sir Edward himself, you mark my words."

Laura was frightened. She glanced at the miniature in the gold frame she always kept on her dressing table. It was a small painting, a very fine likeness of her father. The artist had somehow captured his laughing eyes. Father not cheerful? Father not safe! It was hard to imagine. Still, Laura trembled for him. Mrs. Worthington spoke with authority. She was afraid of the Nailbourne. Somehow, because of the Nailbourne, Parker's brother had died. When Giles had spoken of the Nailbourne, Laura had not been concerned. After all, he was only a superstitious boy. But if Mrs. Worthington was afraid—

Laura sat up in bed. "Martha! Martha!" she called to her maid.

She could not bear being alone another moment. She must know why Mrs. Worthington had said that about Father. What did she mean by saying that no one, not even the master, was safe when the Nailbourne appeared?

20

Martha's frightened face appeared around the door. "Yes, miss."

"Martha, what is it? What is wrong?"

Martha stepped into the room with Mrs. Worthington bustling along behind her. As always, Mrs. Worthington was smiling. One would never know that it was she who only moments before had spoken of the terrible fate of Parker's brother.

"Now, now, it's nothing for you to think about, Miss Laura," she said smoothly, motioning Martha to silence. "Why, this promises to be a lovely day. Your riding clothes are all laid out. You must be quick about dressing. The others are already gathering below."

Mrs. Worthington continued to smile expansively while drawing back the bedclothes.

Laura was not deceived. Something was very wrong. Mrs. Worthington hovered about while Martha helped Laura to dress. Both of them knew something, and both of them were frightened. Laura thought it was obvious in everything they said and did. If it had not been a question of Father's being in danger, Laura might not have been so troubled. She ached to know what was wrong. Perhaps Father must be warned against danger. If only she knew!

Sir Edward met his daughters and Miss Haversmith at the stables. The early-morning air was cool, and the mists still clung to the meadows. Laura had always loved this time of day. Now the very mists seemed threatening. She resolved to ride close to Father.

Sir Edward was in a jovial mood. He was mounted on Morgan, his chestnut stallion, and the other horses were saddled and ready. He greeted his daughters and their governess with a smile.

"Where shall we take Elliot this morning?" he asked.

"What should he see first? When I was a boy, I liked the cove and a ride along the sand beside the sea. I daresay he hasn't seen anything like that."

The cove! Laura felt sure that was where the danger lay. Hadn't she just heard Mrs. Worthington say that Parker's brother had disappeared in the meadow near the cove?

"Oh," she cried. Her voice was high and frightened. "Not the cove, Father."

"Why ever not the cove, my dear?" asked Sir Edward.

Laura took a deep breath before she answered. What could she say? To tell him she was afraid for his safety because of servants' gossip she had overheard sounded ridiculous. Still, she was afraid for Father. "Not even the master is safe," Mrs. Worthington had said.

"I—that is—Couldn't we take Elliot north to Witch's Cottage?"

If pressed, Laura would have to admit that seeing the cone-shaped chimneys that gave the cottage its name was hardly as exciting as Father's suggestion. She sought desperately about for an excuse.

"He might be tired of the sea," she said at last. "He told me yesterday that he had lived in India and that he had traveled all the way to England by ship. He must be tired of the sea."

"Good heavens, what sort of reason is that?" asked Alexandra in disgust. Her black riding clothes were most becoming, and she sat her horse perfectly. She looked at Laura with great disdain.

"The cove and the sea would be lovely, Father," said Alexandra.

Laura was forced to agree. Still, she had the feeling that something dreadful was about to happen.

Miss Haversmith, of course, said nothing but beamed at Alexandra in silent approval.

Elliot, too, applauded the choice when they joined him at the gates of the manor.

"I'd like to see the places my father loved when he was a boy. Do you know, I seem to remember his mentioning a cove and an old, abandoned windmill not far away."

Sir Edward smiled. "It's still there, my boy. All there, and you shall see it."

Laura and her father rode on either side of Elliot, while Miss Haversmith and Alexandra followed along behind. The mists had only just begun to lift. Slowly the thatched roofs of village cottages swam into view. As the sun grew stronger, it became apparent that there would be no rain again that day.

Perhaps that is it, thought Laura. Perhaps it is the drought that depresses me so. Perhaps I only imagine that there is danger. What is wrong with me that I should feel so dismal on a lovely day?

The riders sauntered along the carriageway.

"My father loved the manor, the countryside, and Tonbridge Wells," said Elliot. "He often spoke fondly of his home here. I think he would have been happier if only he might have stayed."

"Why did he leave?" asked Laura.

She could not imagine her own father leaving Covington Castle. It was so much a part of him.

Elliot sighed. "I don't know. He said only that he could never go home again."

"Oh," said Laura. "I am sorry."

She did not know what else to say. She felt she had pried into a personal matter and was embarrassed.

As they rode, they passed a number of farmers in milk carts on their way to Tonbridge Wells. When the men saw Sir Edward, they saluted respectfully, and he nodded and smiled a greeting.

One thing Laura noticed that seemed most curious was that the farmers were riding in pairs. Not one was alone. The first explanation that came to mind was that the villagers were afraid. Oh, if only she dared tell Father what she had heard. Would he think her foolish?

North and east of the village the riders left the road. Father's horse began to gallop, and soon they were all riding swiftly over the meadows toward the hidden cove.

Laura tried to catch up with her father, who was far in the lead. This was much too dangerous. No matter what, she would tell him now. Anything was better than this blind fear. But Laura's pony was no match for Father's stallion and Elliot's fine horse. The farther Sir Edward drew ahead of them, the more uncomfortable Laura became. The sun had burned the mists entirely away, and when the riders reached the cove the air was clear.

The small cove would be difficult to find, if one did not know its exact location. It was enclosed near the water's edge by thick willows whose branches hung down heavily and trailed in the water. On the far side stood the ancient, crumbling windmill.

"Your father and I used to play here, Elliot. There are hundreds of places to hide, as you can see, though I would not recommend the mill. It might fall to pieces at any time. The water isn't really dangerous. It is quite shallow, although at the moment the level does look a bit higher than usual," said Sir Edward.

He began to ride along the shore, studying the water curiously.

"Perhaps it is not so safe at this time as I thought," he added.

"Is it seawater, sir?" asked Elliot.

"Not really. It is fed by underground streams that flow from here into the sea."

Sir Edward stopped to listen.

"That's curious. Do you hear it?"

The sound of running water was quite distinct, and yet the waters of the cove hardly moved.

Sir Edward turned his horse and began to ride away from the shore.

"Why, look here! I do believe we've discovered a Nailbourne."

"A Nailbourne!" cried Laura.

They all looked down and saw a narrow stream which they could easily follow as it wound its way back across the meadows toward Covington Castle in the distance. Why, it was the very stream Giles had pointed out yesterday! Laura should have realized the stream would empty eventually into the cove. Father did not sound in the least disturbed by the discovery, only rather pleased instead.

Elliot looked at Laura as though willing her not to speak. He need not have worried. She wouldn't have given him away.

"What is a Nailbourne?" asked Elliot.

"Nailbournes are underground streams that surface mysteriously from time to time. Rather interesting, actually, and much less mysterious than most people think. We are unique here in Kent, in that we have large chalk deposits beneath the soil. Water can collect beneath the surface for quite some time, and then, when the porous chalk is completely saturated like a sponge, a stream will push its way toward the surface, usually after times of drought. A simple scientific principle explains it all, you see. Shall we have our ride beside the sea and then follow this one back?"

The last thing Laura wanted to do was to follow the "evil waters," but she dared not say anything. Father's explanation had been so sensible. So it was that they followed the stream on their way back. Laura continued to ride close to Father. At least she could do that.

But it was not Father who was in danger. As they neared the outer gardens of the castle, Laura could see the men working already.

The day was growing warm as the sun glowed down upon them. The trees and shrubs looked like cutout forms, so sharply were they etched against the blue of the sky. Laura saw a boy with a wheelbarrow of stones in the distance. From where she was, it looked like Giles, but she could not be sure.

Elliot was sure. Without warning, he dug his heels into his horse's sides and raced off toward the wall, shouting wildly to the gardener's boy.

"Get back!" he yelled. "Get back! Run, I tell you. Run for your life, Giles."

Giles turned slowly, resting the wheelbarrow on a rock. He did not seem to understand. He was so far away he probably could not have heard distinctly.

Elliot galloped forward, shouting again and again, "Run for your life, Giles! Run!"

Sir Edward was alarmed. "What's wrong with the boy? What's he doing?" He started after Elliot.

"Madness will out," said Miss Haversmith darkly and shook her head.

Laura and Alexandra were too surprised to do anything.

Then, while they all watched, a mist welled up from nowhere. In seconds it had completely enveloped Giles. It swirled and spread like a gray wall between them and the boy. All around them was a strange, unearthly hissing sound. Laura heard it. They all heard it. Words that were spoken yesterday came back to Laura.

"Evil waters! Bad times! Poor devil! Poor, poor devil!"

"Father!" cried Laura in sheer panic. "Father!"

Elliot's horse reared and bolted to the left. After fighting to control Morgan, Sir Edward overtook Elliot. The girls and Miss Haversmith followed. Even Alexandra looked pale and shaken when they finally came to a stop.

"Father, what was that?" she demanded.

"Another phenomenon of the Nailbourne, I believe. Possibly some sort of hot spring that suddenly erupts, to everyone's amazement. The warm water sprays up into the cooler air, creating a mist, as you saw. Nothing to be alarmed about. You will find, though, the villagers have a rather terrifying explanation of their own.

"I remember the last time a Nailbourne appeared, more than a dozen years ago. The village was up in arms, terrified. There was no reasoning with anyone. I wouldn't pay a bit of attention to any superstitious talk you might hear among the servants."

Sir Edward turned to Elliot, who had dismounted and was standing beside his trembling horse.

"What made you run off like that?"

Elliot did not reply. He was gazing back at the place where the mists were now rising and hanging like a ragged curtain above the trees and bushes. In the clearing where Giles had been, stood the wheelbarrow of stones, but that was all. There was not a living soul in sight.

Elliot's Dreadful Gift

"The gardener's boy! He's gone! Poor devil," cried Elliot.

His black eyes looked enormous, and for one awful moment Laura thought he would cry.

"Well, but of course he's gone," said Sir Edward. "Terrified I daresay. You ran at him like such a demon, Elliot. No doubt he is cowering on the other side of the wall. Whatever possessed you?"

Elliot stared at the ground and said nothing. What could he say? wondered Laura. What could Elliot tell us, if he cared to? He had known that something was going to happen to Giles. But how? And why didn't Elliot speak?

He refused to say anything all the way back and waved a silent good-by as they left him at the manor.

As soon as the others reached Covington Castle, Father made inquiries. Giles was nowhere to be found in the castle gardens.

"It was the evil waters," Laura overheard Mrs. Worthington tell Martha. "They've taken him the way they've taken others. It won't stop with Giles. You mark my words."

Martha had cried out in fear, and Laura almost did the same, but she dared not give herself away. She was deliberately eavesdropping, for Mrs. Worthington had not been inclined to discuss the Nailbourne or Giles in front of Laura. Laura rather thought Father had instructed the servants not to mention the subject. Father seemed so certain that the waters had nothing to do with Giles's disappearance.

He stubbornly continued to believe that Giles had run away, even though the boy had still not turned up after several days.

Laura, who usually agreed with Father on most everything, found herself questioning him. After all, Father had not seen Elliot that day in the garden. She was convinced that Elliot knew what had happened to Giles and had, in some strange way, known about it beforehand. The thought frightened her, but she longed to be able to talk with Elliot. There had been no opportunity. Since they had left Elliot at the manor that morning, she had not seen him.

"Elliot frightened poor Giles out of his wits," Sir Edward told Lady Caroline. "I can't think why. He couldn't have known those stories about the Nailbourne, could he?"

"I hardly think so," replied Lady Caroline. "He hasn't been here long enough."

"The boy really worries me. Dreadfully nervous child. We must do all we can for him, for his father's sake." Sir Edward frowned. "I wish I could stay about and see to him myself, but I'm wanted in London again."

Lady Caroline rose to the occasion.

"Lady Simpson-Favorite must be beside herself over the boy. I warned her that a child is a terrible burden. But never mind. I shall think of some way to help. I shall take Laura and Alexandra and call on her this very day."

"Ah, that's the spirit, my dear," Sir Edward said cheerfully. "Everything will come right in the end, won't it?"

Laura was pleased to learn that she would at last see Elliot. Almost every morning, they rode past the gates of the manor, but he had not joined them. She had been hoping Mother would suggest a visit.

But Father was going to go away again. Laura felt sadder than usual to hear this news. Sad and a little frightened too. She had never been frightened when Father went away. Whatever was the matter with her?

"How long will you be gone, Father?" she asked anxiously.

"No more than a fortnight, my dear. Of course—" He hesitated and lifted Laura onto his knee. "Of course, there is always the possibility I may be longer."

Laura realized that Father was looking past her at Mother, who unaccountably took that precise moment to prick her finger as she worked on her embroidery.

"Longer?" asked Lady Caroline sharply. "Longer, Edward? Why longer? Is there trouble? One hears such odd things nowadays."

Laura watched Father's face. He answered slowly, as though he were choosing his words carefully. His expression was cheerful enough, but Laura had the impression that he was worried about something.

"Oh, no, no! No trouble! Not really. And if I should be delayed, I would send word to you."

He leaned forward and kissed Laura's forehead.

"Run along now, my dear. I expect Miss Haversmith will be waiting for you. Shall I bring you something special for a surprise this time?"

Reluctantly Laura rose.

"Thank you, Father. I should like that. Only have a good trip. We shall all miss you," she said and hurried from the room. An almost uncontrollable desire to cry had swept over her, and she was terribly ashamed.

What made her so nervous and absentminded lately? Miss Haversmith thought that it was the influence of Elliot's madness and said so several times when Laura had not done well at her lessons. But Laura thought it all went back to the day she had first seen the Nailbourne.

In the afternoon Lady Caroline, dressed in pale blue, and her daughters, both in white, arrived at the manor in time for tea.

Alexandra, a small copy of her mother, sat looking bored while the two ladies talked. To Laura's great disappointment, Elliot was not present.

Lady Simpson-Favorite was distraught.

"Oh, my dear Lady Caroline, I cannot begin to tell you what it has been like. The boy has taken to his room and refuses to come out. We've had the doctor, but he finds nothing wrong. What am I to do?"

"Tell me everything," begged Lady Caroline.

Laura nearly sighed aloud with impatience. She was not in the least interested in the foods Elliot refused to eat. She wanted to see him.

When Lady Simpson-Favorite finally thought to pass the cakes, Laura saw her chance. Though she dearly loved chocolate pastries, she refused them politely and asked if she might see Elliot.

"Perhaps he needs to see another child," she suggested,

32

trying very hard not to seem too anxious. "Perhaps I could cheer him."

Lady Simpson-Favorite put down her teacup and stared at Laura.

"My dear, what a good idea!" she cried. "Would you really try? He does so need cheering."

"Oh, yes," breathed Laura gratefully. "I shall go to him at once, if you like."

Lady Simpson-Favorite turned to Alexandra. "And you, my dear? Would you care to visit Elliot, too?"

Laura's heart sank. If Alexandra came along, how could Elliot possibly talk openly? Laura need not have worried. Alexandra merely looked startled.

"Why, I shouldn't think I'd be any help at all," she said stiffly. "Laura is so much closer in age to dear Elliot."

Lady Simpson-Favorite held her lavender scarf to her eyes for a moment.

"What am I thinking of? You are quite right, Alexandra. Well then, let me ring for Randolph. He'll take Laura to Elliot's side. I am so grateful, child," she added, patting Laura's shoulder with a trembling hand.

It was some minutes before Randolph answered Lady Simpson-Favorite's ring. The butler had been with the family for many years. He was older than Lady Simpson-Favorite herself, and, in addition to his slow, faltering movements, Randolph was terribly hard of hearing. No doubt the other servants had to call the sound of the bell to his attention. But at last he came and led Laura up the long, marble staircase, through the gallery of family portraits, to Elliot's room.

Elliot answered their knock in a weak voice.

"Who is it?"

"Please, it's Laura. Mayn't I come in?"

"Oh," said Elliot.

There was a long pause, and then he shuffled to the door in robe and slippers and opened it only a crack.

"What is it?" he asked.

Laura had only a glimpse of his pale, thin figure and the darkened room.

"I want to talk to you, Elliot," she insisted.

"No, you don't," replied Elliot unhappily. "No one should."

Laura became impatient. Elliot certainly was feeling sorry for himself.

"What a dreadful thing to say! I do want to talk to you and I shall," cried Laura. She pushed the door open firmly and stepped into the room.

She went directly to the heavy curtains that shrouded the windows and pushed them back. The bright sunlight poured in, touching every part of the room and bringing it cheerfully to life. Elliot sank down on the foot of the bed and covered his eyes as though they hurt.

"You should not have done that," he cried.

"Why not? No wonder you are feeling gloomy, sitting alone here in the dark! You'll see. You shall feel much better in a moment," Laura assured him.

"No," said Elliot. "You don't understand." He still sat with his eyes covered.

"Then explain it to me," said Laura, pulling up a chair. "And don't you think you could look at me while we talk?"

"No," said Elliot stubbornly. "That's the very thing I must not do. I must not look at anyone at all."

Laura was completely at a loss. She had never heard of such behavior. For a moment she was almost inclined to

34

agree with Miss Haversmith's opinion of madness, but her instinct told her that this was not the case. She waited patiently for Elliot to explain himself.

"Please, Elliot. Please look at me," she said softly, and at last he did, sighing with relief.

"Thank goodness, you're all right," he said.

"Well, yes, I am just fine," replied Laura in surprise. "It's you who've been ill."

Elliot shook his head. "Not really, I only wish I had been ill. Then there would be medicine to cure me. Oh, it's useless! Useless!" He held his head in his hands.

Laura could not begin to imagine what was wrong. If Elliot were not ill, why was he staying in bed? Laura herself hated to be confined in that way. She could not imagine why Elliot would want to remain in his room voluntarily. But it was obvious something was terribly wrong.

"Please, Elliot, do tell me about it. I'd like to help if I can," she encouraged.

Elliot sighed.

"You'll think me mad," he warned. "Sometimes I think so myself."

"You mustn't," cried Laura. "That's nonsense."

"Is it? I wonder," said Elliot. "I know what they say about my mother. One can't help knowing, and I can hardly blame them. But she wasn't mad. Not at all. It's just that—just that—" Elliot faltered.

"If I am going to be any help at all," said Laura gently, "I must know. Truly, I'll do my best to understand."

Elliot looked into Laura's earnest face and gave in.

"Very well! I warn you. It's a terrible secret and very hard to believe. But I swear to you it's all true."

He rose, strolled to the window and looked out at the

35

bright spring day. He spoke with his back to her, as if it were easier that way.

"You see, I seem to know things, dreadful things, about people. Not all the time, but sometimes. It's happened again and again, only more often as I grow older.

"Take Giles. I knew something awful was going to happen to him. I did not know what, and I still don't, but I knew he was in for trouble. The worst thing was I could not save him."

Elliot paused for a moment as though it were too difficult for him to go on. When he did, his voice was choked with unshed tears.

"I don't want to know anything about anyone anymore. So the best thing is to stay in my room and see no one, not even you. I couldn't bear it if something happened to you."

Elliot turned slowly to face Laura.

"Now do you understand?"

"Oh, Elliot," cried Laura. She stared at him with wide, frightened eyes. Never in her life had she heard a story like this. She could hardly believe her ears, but she must. The only alternative would be that Elliot was mad. She refused to believe that. Besides, she had seen for herself what Elliot's first meeting with Giles had been like. There was no other explanation for Elliot's behavior. It was a terrifying explanation and so utterly sad for Elliot that Laura could think of no words to comfort him.

"So," said Elliot sadly, "you don't believe me. I had hoped that you—" He broke off and bit his lip.

Laura rose instantly from her chair. She held out both hands to Elliot, who took them gratefully.

"Of course I believe you," she cried. "How could I do otherwise? It's just that such a dreadful gift is so—so

36

unusual. Surely there is something that can be done."

Elliot shook his head.

"There is nothing. My mother tried everything. She consulted wise men in India. Still, there was nothing. She had the gift until she died."

Two tears slid unheeded down Laura's cheeks. She had never felt so helpless. If only there were someone they could consult. But Miss Haversmith was all too anxious to believe Elliot mad. And Laura was rather inclined to think the strain would be too much for either Mother or Lady Simpson-Favorite. If only Father had not gone to London.

"You can't shut yourself away in this room forever, Elliot," she said at last, recovering herself a bit.

"What else can I do?"

"But it's awful for you!" insisted Laura.

"Yes," said Elliot quietly.

Both sank down wearily on the window seat.

"I don't think you had better come back to visit after this," said Elliot. "I should enjoy your company, but it would be better if you didn't come."

Laura was hardly listening. The beginning of an idea was forming in her mind. At last she turned shining eyes to Elliot.

"Has it ever occurred to you that your strange gift could help prevent disasters?"

"Naturally," said Elliot, smiling wanly. "I tried to save Giles. You saw what happened."

"But, Elliot, you were trying to do it all alone. What if there were others to help you?" Laura's voice rose with excitement.

"Who would believe me?"

"I already do. And then there's Father. Elliot, if you

could help people with your gift, it would all be worth-while, wouldn't it?"

"I suppose so," said Elliot doubtfully.

Laura leaped to her feet. "Then that's it," she said. "We must begin at once. The first thing would be to get out and about."

Elliot tried to protest, but Laura would not listen.

"Shall I wait in the gallery while you dress?"

She was determined to have her way.

"All right," agreed Elliot reluctantly. "Perhaps it is worth a try after all."

Laura found the gallery most interesting. It was a nar-row hallway lined on one side with long windows that allowed light to fall on the family portraits. There were many of them, beginning with the first Lord Elliot Simp-son-Favorite who had defended his country so valiantly during an invasion that he had been rewarded by the King with the magnificent manor house and all the lands about it.

There was a splendid portrait of Lady Simpson-Favor-ite herself when she was much, much younger. Laura was surprised to find how very lovely the old woman had been. She had once had rich black hair and beautiful dark eyes. Laura could not have recognized her except that Lady Simpson-Favorite's name was engraved on a small copper plate.

The last portrait was of Elliot's father. There was a striking resemblance between father and son. The large black eyes seemed identical.

Laura was most interested in the next to the last paint-ing of two children, a boy and a girl. There was something about their small, pinched faces that kept them from look-ing like children at all. Their mouths were straight and thin, and there was not even a hint of a smile. Discontent! That was it. Discontent was their most striking feature.

Elliot, dressed and looking more confident, joined her before this picture.

"My father's half brother and half sister," he explained. "Twins, as you can see. My grandmother married twice. These are the children of her first marriage, Uncle George and Aunt Georgina Tonner. Father did not get on with them at all. I had the impression that they were the reason he could not return home. Why that should be, I do not know. Shall we join the others? I feel so much better now, thanks to you."

He smiled, and it was a pleasure to see him so cheerful again.

"Together we shall be able to do something. I know it, Elliot. Yes, let's join the others. I do hope there are some chocolate cakes left. I am awfully fond of chocolate, aren't you?"

In the drawing room the ladies were still chatting over their tea when Laura and Elliot joined them.

Lady Simpson-Favorite was delighted when she saw her grandnephew up and about.

"My darling boy!" she cried. "Are you feeling better then? Oh, Lady Caroline, your daughter is a wonder! How can I ever thank you, Laura dear? Do sit down and have some cakes, both of you."

Lady Simpson-Favorite looked with dismay at the empty tray. "Why, we've eaten them all. Just fancy! But never mind! Never mind! I shall ring for more."

When Randolph finally brought the cakes, he was obviously disturbed. He had to steady himself by leaning on the back of a chair before setting down the tray.

"I am sorry, madam. Please forgive me."

39

"Randolph, what is the matter?" demanded Lady Simpson-Favorite. "Are you ill?" she asked loudly.

Randolph's pale lips trembled.

"Begging your pardon, my lady," he said. "We've just had bad news from the village. You will remember the gardener's boy from Covington Castle. Giles, they called him."

"Giles!" gasped Laura without thinking.

"Yes, oh, yes," said Lady Simpson-Favorite. "Disappeared, didn't he? You must have been dreadfully distressed, dear Lady Caroline," she said, turning to her friend.

"Yes, indeed," said Laura's mother.

Laura found the suspense nearly unbearable. Why didn't Randolph tell them the news?

"Well, Randolph, what has happened? Have they found poor Giles?"

"No, my lady, I'm afraid not. There is no sign of him. And now two more men have disappeared. The villagers think it is the work of the—the Devil, my lady. The Nailbourne is back."

"The Nailbourne!" cried Lady Simpson-Favorite. "The Nailbourne again, Lady Caroline. What is to be done?"

Laura glanced at Elliot, but he only shook his head and looked as surprised as everyone else. Evidently this time he had not known a thing.

More Disasters

Lady Caroline felt she must visit the families of the missing men. Giles had been an orphan, living at the gardener's cottage, but the other young men had left families who were in need of help.

"We must bring them comfort and courage. It is our duty," Lady Caroline told her daughters several days after the disappearance of the men. "You will both accompany me."

For generations the Covingtons had not done less for the villagers. When illness or tragedy struck, a visit from the lady of the castle was in order.

"Mrs. Worthington, we must learn what we can about these families," Laura heard her mother direct the housekeeper.

Mrs. Worthington returned with the news in less than an hour.

"Pitiful, my lady. Pitiful! Young Harry Page left a wife expecting their first child. And Robert Bombray was the only son of Widow Bombray. Two women alone now with no one to support and protect them. They'll need food, of

41

course, and the young Mrs. Page will want clothes for the baby to come, poor thing."

Early the next morning Mother ordered the carriage. Harper loaded it with two large baskets of food. Laura peeked beneath the snowy-white cloths. There were jars of currant jelly and calves' foot jelly. There were ham and chicken, fresh rolls and tiny cakes. There were, in addition, two large hampers of clothes, both with things suitable for grown women. One included tiny, lace-trimmed, linen garments for the baby to come.

Laura and Alexandra sat on either side of their mother as the carriage rolled along the sunlit road. Still, it had not rained. The day was lovely. On such a day anyone might be happy. Laura had the oppressive feeling that few people in Tonbridge Wells were happy. Tragedy had struck and might strike again.

Overhead the new green leaves of tall oak trees formed a canopy. Alexandra and Lady Caroline sat quietly, glancing neither to the left, nor to the right. They seemed not to notice the sad-faced men and women who stopped by the side of the road and bowed respectfully as the carriage passed. Laura's heart went out to them. She wished somehow to comfort them, but what could she do?

Laura tried her best to imitate her mother's composure, but her bright-blue eyes were alert, and she could not help seeing the frightened faces of the villagers. They all guessed the tragic reason for Lady Covington's visit. Wives stood beside their husbands as if their presence could protect the men and keep them from disappearing so mysteriously.

Laura was struck with a thought. Only men seemed to disappear. Why only men? She wondered if anyone knew.

"Why is it only men who disappear, Mother?" she

asked aloud, curiosity having gotten the better of her tongue.

Lady Caroline looked down at her daughter in surprise. "What a question, child! Who can know the answer?"

Laura did not find this a satisfactory reply, but her mother did not seem inclined to elaborate. Laura decided to discuss it with Elliot. Might not his unusual gift help him to know what no one else knew?

The carriage stopped first at the cottage of Mrs. Page. The young woman was obviously expecting them. She met Harper at the door, glanced at the two large hampers gratefully and then at Lady Covington. The young widow curtsied awkwardly and lowered her eyes.

"Oh, my lady! You are too kind. How can I thank you?"

Lady Caroline swept into the one-room cottage with Alexandra and Laura following close behind. Inside, the room was dim after the bright sunlight. There was only one small shuttered window. Laura found she had to wait patiently for her eyes to get used to the sudden change in light. The room, she saw at last, was sparsely furnished with a wooden table, two chairs, and a straw pallet on a wooden plank for a bed.

Mother and Alexandra sat on the chairs and Laura stood, while Mrs. Page served them cups of weak tea, which no one drank.

"Now, my dear, tell me how it happened," said Mother.

Mrs. Page sat down on the edge of the bed. She had pale yellow hair wound in a smooth braid about her head. Her large eyes were swollen from crying.

"He went out to bring in the sheep as he always does. They graze on the common meadow by the old windmill. I watched him go until I couldn't see him for the trees. Oh, he was a fine figure of a man, he was, my lady. There was no stronger man in the village than my Harry."

The young woman faltered, took a deep breath, and recovered herself.

"Well, that's all! He didn't come back. No one has seen him since. He's gone—gone for good. My baby will never know his father. Why did they take my Harry? Those devil waters!"

Mrs. Page buried her face in her apron and began to weep.

Laura was terribly moved. Her heart filled with compassion for this poor young wife. Laura felt she, too, would have begun to weep had it not been for Mother's brisk, confident voice.

"There, there, my dear. You must not give up hope. You must think of your child."

Mrs. Page managed to control herself. When her guests were ready to leave, she saw them to the door, thanking Lady Caroline all the while for her kindness.

"Poor creature," remarked Mother sadly when they were once more settled in their carriage. "I wish there were something more we could do."

"Perhaps Mrs. Worthington could find a place for Mrs. Page in our kitchen until the baby comes," suggested Alexandra, who was holding a perfumed handkerchief to her nose. She was extremely sensitive to all kinds of odors. Those in the peasant cottages were particularly strong. Laura thought her sister would probably take to her bed with a headache before the day was over.

"A place in the kitchen for Mrs. Page! Now, that is a thought," said Lady Caroline, considerably cheered. "How clever of you, Alexandra!" she added, patting her daughter's white-gloved hand.

"It seems to me," said Laura, "that it would be far better to find Harry Page himself."

Alexandra cast a disdainful glance at her sister, and their mother greeted Laura's suggestion with little enthusiasm.

"Laura dear, that is easier said than done. You are too young to remember the last time, when fourteen men disappeared. Your father has always thought it best that you children not be frightened by the superstitions of the villagers. That is why the coming of the Nailbourne has never been discussed with you. Your father is convinced the stories of devil waters possessing our men are nonsense. However, he himself was unable to find the men the last time, although he tried very hard.

"It is best, then, not to think too much of the mystery and try to do what we can for those women who are left alone. It is what your father would want."

Laura could tell from her mother's tone that the subject was closed. There were so many other things Laura wanted to know, but dared not ask. She was glad to know that Father had tried to find the men. Perhaps he would do so again and be successful.

The carriage drove on to the home of Widow Bombray, where they heard the now-familiar story of sudden disappearance. Young Robert had gone out late in the afternoon to find and milk the two cows, which had been grazing. He had not come home.

The Widow Bombray was the saddest person Laura had ever seen. All the lines in her old face turned down. And no wonder!

"Poor Robert has gone the way of his father," the widow told Lady Caroline. "Not twelve years ago his father was taken the same way. The village is cursed by the evil waters. The Nailbourne comes, the devil mists rise and take our men."

As Laura listened, she remembered the morning on the meadow when Giles had disappeared. Mists had risen up. Though Father had an explanation for them, Giles had vanished. Giles and the others!

Mother said that Father did not believe the story of devil waters. But if devils had not stolen the men, who had? Laura could imagine no other explanation than a kind of evil magic.

It was a relief to leave the widow's cottage. In the bright, yellow sunshine the terrifying idea seemed unreal. It was a pleasure to go home again where everything was calm and orderly. Laura did not even mind her lessons the next morning, though the arithmetic was getting harder than ever. Besides, she was looking forward to the afternoon, when Lady Simpson-Favorite and Elliot were coming to call.

As soon as they arrived, Laura took Elliot to sit and talk in the garden house. Laura told him about the visits.

"It was all so sad. I've been thinking about it ever since. There must be some way your gift could help. Elliot, have you no idea what might have happened to the men yourself?"

Elliot shook his head. "I cannot begin to guess. How could I? You sound as if you thought I did know and was keeping the information to myself. I would not do that, you may be sure."

Elliot sounded hurt, and Laura quickly tried to soothe him.

"Of course, I didn't mean that. Not at all. It just might be that you're overlooking something. For instance, when you see things—that is, know things—is there nothing

46

more than the feeling of disaster, or do you know what kind of disaster?"

Elliot hesitated.

"It's like suddenly seeing a picture. For a few seconds I seem to—to lose track of where I am. I see another place entirely. Instead of what is, I see what will be. It's like having a glimpse of the future, but only a glimpse. It's just awful! I always try to put it out of my mind as quickly as possible."

"But you mustn't!" cried Laura. "Not if we are to help. We must know all that we can. Try to remember now. Think back to Giles. What actually did you see?"

Elliot gave her an odd look and then leaned forward, his elbows on his knees, his head bowed in his hands. He gave a shuddering sigh, and his words came slowly, as though he were seeing it all again.

"I saw him in chains. And—and there seemed to be a fire. A terrible fire somewhere nearby!"

"Oh," said Laura softly.

Elliot's description sounded suspiciously like Vicar Dorchester's warnings of suffering souls in hellfire. Only last Sunday his eloquent words had moved members of the small congregation at St. John's Church to tears. Now Laura almost wished she had not asked Elliot to tell her anything. Perhaps the plight of the missing men was as hopeless as everyone believed.

"It isn't much help, is it?" asked Elliot, without looking at her. "I suppose it's only made things worse for you, for both of us."

"Well . . ." began Laura, but she did not finish. She could think of nothing else to say. She thought there was nothing in what Elliot had said that could be used to help Giles. For a long time neither of them spoke.

All about the gardens birds called cheerily from tree to tree. A flock of yellow jonquils waved in the gentle breeze, and Elliot's terrible vision began to recede.

"I know where there is a good tree for climbing," said Elliot, suddenly jumping to his feet.

Laura was startled at first by this sudden change of mood. But then she saw in his face that Elliot was forcing himself to be cheerful.

"Shall we try it?" he asked.

"Oh, yes," replied Laura, wanting to help him all she could. What a burden his terrible gift must be! "Where is this tree?"

"The old flowering crabapple in the walled garden. The branches are low, and one might gain a foothold on the wall to begin."

"All right," said Laura with enthusiasm. At least for a time they could forget the tragedies of Tonbridge Wells. She led the way along the paths through carefully tended yew hedges. The tree Elliot had selected was in full bloom, a mass of pink-and-white blossoms.

The children scrambled up the gray stones of the inner wall. From the top, Elliot was able to step easily onto the first strong branch, which shook slightly with his weight, sending a shower of delicate petals to the ground. When he had made his way close to the trunk and onto a second, higher branch, he motioned to Laura to follow. Feeling adventurous and a little guilty about this probably forbidden pleasure, Laura obeyed. What would Miss Haversmith say if she could see Laura now? Twigs tugged at her hair and tiny pink blossoms dotted her chestnut curls. Once she nearly lost her footing and clung desperately to

48

the trunk, laughing all the while. But when she was seated on a sturdy branch and took time to brush away the tiny pieces of bark from her clothes, she found a long, telltale tear in her pinafore. How she would be able to explain that to her governess, she did not know.

"Well," said Elliot, who had settled on the branch above her. "What do you think of it? Climbing, I mean."

"Marvelous," answered Laura happily.

From her position she could look back over the gardens to the terrace where the ladies were having tea. Alexandra was there too. Poor things! How dull to have to sit sedately, holding your teacup just so and chatting politely. Here one was free!

Laura breathed deeply the lovely scents of the garden. She looked up through the branches at the clear blue sky and the golden sunlight. She felt part of it, part of the tree, the sky, and the perfumed air. Bees hummed busily about the blossoms. Below, lavender wisteria lined the wall.

"Look!" cried Elliot. "There's a horseman!"

"Where?" asked Laura, squinting up at him.

"There!" Elliot was pointing away from the castle gardens toward the meadows. Laura had to shift her position to see.

Good heavens! There was the Nailbourne again. In her pleasure and excitement, Laura had nearly forgotten it. The day was warm, and yet she shuddered at the sight of the mystery waters. They bubbled softly through the meadows, meandering slowly, curving past the garden wall and moving toward the circle of trees that hid the small cove from sight. Beside the stream a man was riding a splendid white horse toward the hidden cove.

Laura glanced up at Elliot.

"Should he—Should he be there?"

No sheep or cows were grazing in the meadow that day. No doubt the villagers had found another, safer place for their livestock.

"I don't know," replied Elliot. "I don't feel anything. Perhaps he is all right. Who is he, do you suppose?"

Soft laughter drew Laura's attention instantly to the ground below. She looked down to see her maid, Martha, gazing up at her with amusement and wonder.

"Miss Laura, what are you doing up there? Miss Haversmith is looking for you everywhere."

"Is she?" asked Laura, trying her best to appear dignified in this unseemly position. "Well, you can tell her I shall be along presently," Laura said calmly.

But she made no move to climb down as yet. She had no intention of allowing Martha to see what must necessarily be uncertain efforts to descend the tree without falling. She was not altogether sure she could do it at all, much less gracefully.

Martha stood waiting.

"Is there something else?" asked Laura briskly. Why didn't Martha go?

"Lady Simpson-Favorite went back to the manor, miss. She said for Master Elliot to follow. They expect visitors."

"Visitors? I wonder who," said Elliot.

"Thank you, Martha. You may go now," said Laura. And the girl did go reluctantly. She seemed to want to say something more.

With Elliot's help Laura managed nicely.

"Why don't you borrow my pony to ride home?" suggested Laura. "It will be quicker, and you can bring him back tomorrow."

Laura brushed apple blossoms from her hair and

50

rubbed ineffectually at her soiled pinafore. Her only hope was to slip upstairs and change before she saw Miss Haversmith.

"Thank you," said Elliot. "I've had a lovely afternoon."

He did look well. The exercise had done him good. There was color in his cheeks.

At the stables Laura called to Peters to saddle her pony. The young man obeyed quickly and led the pony out for Elliot to mount. But Elliot did not move. He was staring at Peters in horror.

The young stable boy did not notice. He bent to assist Elliot.

"Here you go, sir," he said.

Laura gazed from Elliot to Peters, her heart beating wildly. Something was going to happen to Peters, and Elliot knew about it.

The Unexpected Visitors

"I've changed my mind," said Elliot. "I shall walk."

He turned and strode away so quickly that it was moments before Laura was able to catch up with him. Peters stared after them both in surprise.

"Do wait, Elliot. Please!" cried Laura. She was quite out of breath by the time they had reached the approach to the castle.

Elliot slowed his pace, and she was able to walk beside him.

"We can save Peters this time. We can," she assured him.

Elliot stopped walking and turned to face her.

"How?" he demanded.

"Tell him," said Laura promptly.

"No," said Elliot.

"But why?"

"Because he wouldn't believe me. He'd only laugh behind my back and think me mad."

"Oh, Elliot, not after the others have disappeared. He would very likely know that he could be next. Let us go back. We can at least try," she begged.

"No," said Elliot. "How can I tell the poor fellow he is doomed and offer him no hope? How can I warn him to avoid something that is nameless? Don't you see what that would do to him? And it wouldn't help at all. Oh, it's no use. It's no use!"

He started to hurry off again.

"Elliot, please. You promised. You said we would try to prevent disasters together."

Elliot stopped walking then, but he stood with his back to her.

"At least tell me what you saw," she insisted.

"Something simply burned and blew up. Peters was in the middle of it. I think it was a building."

"A building? What building? Elliot, don't you see? If we knew what building, that would be a start. You could tell Peters to avoid it."

"I don't know what building. I don't know," shouted Elliot angrily, turning to face her. "Can't you see? I don't want to think about it!"

He caught his breath. It was almost a sob.

"If you won't think about it, how can we possibly help Peters?" demanded Laura sternly.

She felt she understood how difficult this was for Elliot. But if he did not allow himself to think about what he had seen, how could his gift ever be of any use at all?

Elliot's shoulders sagged, and he shook his head wearily. "Of course you are right," he said. "What do you think I ought to do?"

"Try to remember what building. Describe it. Perhaps if it is near here, I would know what it was."

"All right. All right," said Elliot. He closed his eyes,

then opened them after a few seconds. "It's no use. I can't see anything now."

"I have an idea," cried Laura. "Let's go back to the stables. We'll tell Peters you've decided to ride after all. When you see him again, perhaps there will be something else."

"But I've never done that," protested Elliot. "That is, I've never deliberately tried. Perhaps it won't work."

"Perhaps it will," insisted Laura. "You'll never know unless you try. Poor Peters! You must try."

"Yes," agreed Elliot. "Poor Peters!"

The groom was surprised when the young mistress and master returned. He had just unsaddled the pony and was asked to saddle it once more. The expression on his round, sunburned face was one of confusion, but he obeyed willingly, listening all the while to Laura's cheerful chatter. He hardly noticed Elliot, who was standing apart and concentrating very hard on something no one else could see. His thin features were tense, and his hands were clenched as he made every effort to learn something—anything that might help save Peters.

Once mounted on the pony with the groom's help, Elliot looked down at Peters and spoke so earnestly that the young fellow was nearly alarmed.

"Do you often go into the village, Peters?"

"Once a week, sir, to visit my mother, and any time the master sends me I go."

"And where does your mother live?"

"She has a place at the vicarage, sir, and I visit her there."

"Ah," said Elliot, as if this information were terribly important. "When will you be going again?"

"On Sunday eve, I expect, sir," answered Peters, his wide forehead wrinkled in bewilderment. "She waits on me then usually."

"Yes, I see," said Elliot. "Thank you, Peters," he added briskly and urged the pony forward.

When they were far enough away not to be heard, Elliot dismounted and stood beside Laura. He was pale and obviously shaken.

"We must go into the village," he told her. "I think I would know the building if I saw it. It is nothing that I have seen here. I suspect it is something like a church. But I must see for myself. If Peters remains here until Sunday, I believe he will be safe. Is there much chance that he will be sent into town before that?"

Laura shook her head. "I don't think so. Father isn't home, and Mother probably would not have occasion to go."

"Good," said Elliot. "Then I shall ask Aunt Madelaine to let us ride in tomorrow afternoon. I expect you have lessons in the morning."

At the thought of lessons Laura remembered that Miss Haversmith had sent word for her to return some time ago. Her governess must be very impatient by now and would be waiting to scold. Laura did not see how she could hide her disheveled appearance, even if she hurried, and that would only add to her difficulties.

There was no time for further confidences. She was anxious to learn what Elliot suspected, but she knew she must go. For everyone's sake she hoped that the terrible gift which Elliot possessed might now prove useful. Elliot promised to come for her the next afternoon, and they parted hurriedly.

No one could have said that Miss Haversmith was anything but sedate and proper. She was as little given to fancy and frivolity as anyone Laura had ever known. But that evening there was a sudden and very decided change in the governess.

When Laura returned to her room, she did not find Miss Haversmith waiting as she had expected. Instead, there was only Martha.

"Oh, miss, you are a sight!" cried the maid. "How she'll scold!" Martha nodded in the direction of Miss Haversmith's room.

"I know," said Laura unhappily. Hastily she pulled off the torn pinafore and tossed it aside. Her stockings, too, were in a most dreadful condition. She removed these and finally decided to change her dress as well. It would not do for Miss Haversmith to see any of the clothes Laura had been wearing while tree-climbing.

"I'll dress for dinner now and then see what Miss Haversmith wants," decided Laura. "I am so late already, a few more minutes can't matter. Do you know what it is, Martha?"

"No, miss, I don't," admitted the girl, as she brushed Laura's hair until the curls were all smoothly in place and the chestnut color shone in the candlelight. "But someone did bring a letter for her."

Laura bathed, then raised her arms so that Martha could help with the pale-green silk dress. There were ruffles of white lace about the collar and cuffs. It was quite becoming. Laura admired herself in the looking glass while Martha tied the sash.

Laura wished Father were there to see her now. He would be proud of her. She glanced at the miniature on her dressing table and pretended for a moment that Father was there and that his smile in the picture was one of approval. How she wished he would come home soon!

"A letter?" asked Laura. "Someone brought Miss Haversmith a letter?"

On second thought Miss Haversmith's receiving a letter was really quite curious. She seemed to have no friends or relatives with whom she kept in contact. Miss Haversmith always gave the impression of being a singularly lonely person. A letter would be quite an event. It nearly displaced all thoughts of Peters and the mysterious, impending fire and explosion.

The novelty of the letter was nothing to the novelty of Miss Haversmith's behavior. Dressed and composed, Laura crossed the hall to her governess' room. She would have knocked, but the door was slightly ajar, and Laura was so startled by Miss Haversmith's behavior that she entirely forgot to knock.

The governess was in the center of the room with her back to the door. Her dark hair had been unwound from its accustomed tight knot at the back of her neck. The thick waves fell gracefully about her shoulders and reached to her waist. Most remarkable of all, Miss Haversmith was holding a bright-red taffeta dress to her shoulders and dancing with it. Yes, actually dancing. She hummed and swayed, whirling around at last to see Laura.

Miss Haversmith's cheeks were flushed prettily, and there was a softness about her usually sharp eyes that made her look rather lovely.

"Why, Miss Haversmith, how pretty you look!" cried Laura without thinking, so great was her surprise.

The color in Miss Haversmith's cheeks deepened, for she had been discovered in an unseemly attitude. But she recovered quickly, ignoring Laura's compliment.

58

"Laura!" she cried. "I sent for you more than an hour ago. You have completely missed your tea!"

Miss Haversmith hurriedly tossed her red gown onto the bed and grasped the rich hair that hung becomingly about her shoulders, then twisted it so that it became smooth and taut once more. "Surely by now you must know that good manners require you to knock before entering a room."

Miss Haversmith's eyes blazed angrily. She had evidently forgotten her moment of gay abandon and was warming to the subject at hand. Her sharp features had resumed their pinched, disdainful look. "How can you explain your disobedience?"

Laura gazed down at the floor.

"I don't know, Miss Haversmith. I am sorry if I inconvenienced you."

"Inconvenienced me! You are sorry!"

Miss Haversmith's shocked tone indicated this was hardly enough. "I am afraid this requires a lesson, young miss. I shall have to confine you to your rooms tomorrow afternoon. There will be no frolicking in the gardens with that strange boy "

Laura opened her mouth to protest. How could she and Elliot search for the building he had seen if she was confined to her room? But Miss Haversmith silenced Laura with a look. There could be no appeal now.

"Young lady, your mother has requested that you, Alexandra, and I dine with her this evening. At least you are suitably attired for that. Now go to your room until you are sent for and employ your time with the sums you found so difficult this morning."

Laura turned and walked slowly back to her room. The

punishment itself was not excessive. But what a time for it to come! If Elliot were to save Peters, he needed assistance, her assistance.

She must get word to him. Miss Haversmith was confining Laura to her rooms, but nothing had been said of visitors. Perhaps Elliot might be allowed to come there. Elliot would have to stop by tomorrow in any case to return the pony. Laura must send a message at once. She looked about for some paper.

Laura's room adjoined the schoolroom on the right, while Alexandra's adjoined it on the left. There were doors to both the hall and the schoolroom from the girls' rooms. Laura stepped from her room into the schoolroom in search of her copybook and was just in time to see the door to Alexandra's room closing.

"Alexandra," called Laura, hurrying toward the closed door.

Alexandra was extremely orderly and would certainly have notepaper on hand.

"Yes, what is it?" asked Alexandra.

Laura started and whirled about. There was Alexandra sitting in a high-backed chair by the fire. She held a book in her hands and had obviously been reading.

"Alexandra," cried Laura. "What are you doing there? I thought I just saw you go into your room through that door. Someone certainly closed it just now."

She pointed to the far end of the room.

"Nonsense," said Alexandra in a bored tone. "What has got into you? Surely you are not going to become nervous and fanciful like that dreadful boy."

Alexandra's remark forced Laura's attention from the mysteriously closed door.

"There's nothing dreadful about Elliot," cried Laura

60

indignantly. "He is a splendid person."

"I daresay you are the only one who thinks so," said Alexandra, and she yawned.

Laura found Alexandra particularly trying that evening. Really it must be awful to find everything in life so dull.

Laura gave her sister an appraising glance. Alexandra's appearance was quite lovely as usual. The blue taffeta dress set off her creamy skin and reddish hair to perfection. If she would smile only once in a while! But the perfect features of Alexandra's beautiful face were hardly ever marred or lighted by any expression at all. In many ways Alexandra was very like their governess. How pleasant it would be if Alexandra and Miss Haversmith were to allow themselves to express emotions other than boredom.

If only Miss Haversmith could always look as gay as she had in the moments when Laura surprised her. What could have caused such a change? Laura smiled, remembering.

"What, may I ask, is so amusing?" asked Alexandra.

"Miss Haversmith dancing," said Laura "Dancing with her hair down."

"Oh," cried Alexandra, closing her eyes and shaking her head. "Now I know you are going mad."

"Indeed, I am not," said Laura with dignity. "Not ten minutes ago I saw her in her room, holding up a scarlet gown and dancing."

The idea of Miss Haversmith doing any such thing was so unlikely that Laura might have begun to doubt her own senses had not Miss Haversmith come into the schoolroom an hour later wearing the very gown Laura had described. It was trimmed with white fur and fell in graceful folds to the floor. In it Miss Haversmith looked elegant. Her hair was done differently, too. It was not, of course, loose, but it was piled high on her head in soft loops and waves. Why, she is almost as pretty as Mother, thought Laura.

Alexandra was obviously stunned by the transformation. Laura noted with satisfaction that her sister rose so suddenly from her chair that her book fell to the floor.

"Do be more careful, Alexandra," admonished Miss Haversmith. "Come, young ladies, we must not keep your mother and her guests waiting," she went on in a more pleasant tone.

Laura detected excitement and anticipation in her governess' voice. It was seldom that Miss Haversmith consented to dine with the family, although she was often asked.

"Guests?" asked Laura.

"The Simpson-Favorites and the Tonners are joining us this evening," said Miss Haversmith. "Had you come when I sent for you, Laura, you might have known that."

What good fortune! Elliot would be at dinner. Laura could explain everything to him then. But who were the Tonners? The name seemed vaguely familiar.

Laura needed only to glimpse the faces of the man and woman who were speaking with Mother in the drawing room, to recognize them. The portrait in the gallery at the manor had been painted when they were only children, but the resemblance was striking. They were George and Georgina Tonner, the half brother and half sister of Elliot's father.

Laura and Alexandra were introduced and curtsied politely. Miss Haversmith was also presented.

Laura noticed that Elliot watched his aunt and uncle closely. He soon drew Laura aside.

"There is something wrong here," he whispered. "Miss Haversmith and the Tonners already know each other. I can feel it. Why are they pretending otherwise?"

Suddenly Laura remembered the letter Miss Haversmith had received. Perhaps it had been sent by one of the Tonners.

A Ghostly Intruder

"How did you find India, Mr. Tonner?" asked Lady Caroline as the fish was being served.

Mr. Tonner looked up from his plate and smiled wanly.

"Ah, as usual, Lady Caroline. India, Burma, Siam! They are all alike."

Laura glanced across the table and tried to catch Elliot's eye. Surely he did not think such exotic places were boring. But Elliot seemed to be concentrating on his food. He looked at no one.

Laura turned her attention to Mr. Tonner. He could not be called a handsome man. His eyes were small, and his nose too short and wide, rather like a snout, thought Laura. But his voice was attractive. It was deep and resonant.

"I would trade all the riches of the East for the pleasure of one evening in such lovely company as this," he said, smiling and beaming at the ladies and most especially at Miss Haversmith, who quickly glanced away. Laura had never seen her governess so flustered.

"Had we been able to afford to stay, Georgina and I

would never have left England. All we have ever held dear is right here in Tonbridge Wells. But beggars can't be choosers, as they say, and those of us without family fortunes must make our own, mustn't we?" he added, giving Lady Simpson-Favorite a significant glance.

Lady Simpson-Favorite was sitting in Father's place at the table. As usual she was dressed in shades of lavender and purple. She looked quite regal, and the diamond necklace she wore glittered brilliantly whenever she moved. She seemed surprised to the point of embarrassment by Mr. Tonner's remark.

"But, my dear George, you are always welcome here," she protested. "This is your home. You and Georgina," she told them graciously.

Georgina Tonner was very like her twin brother except for her long dark hair, which she wore in a bun, and the fact that she did not smile so often. Her expression could only be described as sullen.

"When we learned that poor dear Elliot had died and Aunt Madelaine was not in the best of health, of course we had to return. It was our duty," she said virtuously. "Then there is young Elliot here. Poor child," she added. Her expression showed that Elliot's position was, in her eyes, most pitiful.

Elliot shifted uncomfortably under the weight of this unwanted sympathy, but it was Lady Simpson-Favorite who voiced the protest.

"My dear Georgina, Elliot and I are getting on very well. There is no need for your concern. No need whatsoever," said Lady Simpson-Favorite.

Miss Tonner simply ignored this remark.

"There, there, Aunt Madelaine. We know exactly how difficult it has been, and we mean to help," she said with

65

determination. It was obvious to Laura that the Tonners were planning to force their assistance upon the Simpson-Favorites whether it was needed or not. That Elliot found their solicitous attitude completely offensive was quite obvious too. Laura longed for an opportunity to speak with him. She had the impression that he was not in the least fond of these relatives. Hadn't he said as much the day she had discovered their portraits?

"How is your dear husband, Lady Caroline?" inquired Miss Tonner. "We have not met in years. Is he as handsome as ever?"

"He is quite well, thank you," said Lady Caroline. "Alexandra, do pass your locket to Miss Tonner. It contains a recent miniature," she explained to her guest.

Alexandra reached up to unclasp her necklace and cried out in dismay.

"Why, I am not wearing the locket, Mother," she said. "I thought that I was. I always do. Where could it be?"

"No doubt you left it on your dressing table," said Miss Haversmith.

Lady Caroline turned to one of the servants. "Send to Miss Alexandra's room and have her locket brought to us from the dressing table."

"It won't be found there."

Everyone was startled by Elliot's sudden, positive statement.

"I beg your pardon," said Lady Caroline.

They all turned to stare at Elliot. He looked flushed and anxious. Laura could tell he was sorry he had spoken. It must have been an uncontrollable impulse. Now there was nothing for it but to carry on.

"The locket is not on the dressing table. It is hanging

on a hook in the butler's pantry, beneath some sort of white cloth."

"What utter nonsense!" said Alexandra. "I have never been to the butler's pantry."

"Still," said Elliot unhappily, "the locket will be found there."

And it was! Only minutes later a footman returned, carrying the locket.

"What does this mean?" cried Lady Simpson-Favorite. Her dark eyes were wide. "Elliot, how could you know such a thing? What could you possibly be doing in the butler's pantry?"

"I've never been there, Aunt Madelaine," said Elliot.

The misery in his eyes might easily be mistaken for guilt, thought Laura. Poor Elliot! How could she help him?

"But my child, you knew where the locket was! You must have seen it there."

"I did see it," admitted Elliot.

"There, that's better," said Lady Simpson-Favorite, beginning to look relieved. "Just tell us how you happened to be there." She nodded reassuringly at the others. "Elliot can explain it all."

"You don't understand, Aunt Madelaine," said Elliot. "I was never in the butler's pantry. I—I saw the necklace in—in my mind," he finished painfully.

For a moment no one spoke. Instead, they simply stared at Elliot, as though his extraordinary words were not to be believed. Unable to bear it another moment, Elliot rose and ran from the dining room.

"Mother, mayn't I go after him?" pleaded Laura.

"Yes, do," said her mother, staring in disbelief at the

doorway through which Elliot had disappeared.

"Oh, this is too much! Too much!" mourned Lady Simpson-Favorite.

"Is it the madness?" asked Miss Tonner in alarm.

"Is it?" repeated Mr. Tonner, who sounded more interested than alarmed. He was gazing at Miss Haversmith as though he expected her to have the answer. "After all, his mother was not at all normal, you know. Isn't the boy responsible either?"

If Laura had not been so anxious to find and comfort Elliot, she might have taken more notice of Mr. Tonner's shocking attitude. He actually sounded pleased.

Laura at last found Elliot in the library. He was standing before the long windows, looking into the darkening gardens.

"Whatever possessed you, Elliot? If only you had not spoken just then! None of them understands at all," said Laura, coming to stand beside him.

"I know," said Elliot sadly. "I will pay dearly for this mistake. Uncle George will see to that."

"What kind of person is Mr. Tonner?" asked Laura.

"My father detested him," said Elliot. "The last time they were here together, Father and Uncle George must have had a terrible row. They never spoke to each other after that. Once in India, when Father was supervising the family plantations, Uncle George came to him for a loan. Father gave the money to him, but he asked Mother to meet with Uncle George instead of going himself. I remember he said, 'Tell him I don't expect any of it back. Tell him to take the money and go. I never want to see him again.' I was very young at the time, but I can remember the look of loathing on Father's face. I wonder why Uncle George decided to come back now."

68

"Whatever the reason, it cannot concern us," said Laura. "Elliot, what do you know about the locket?"

"You don't think I had anything to do with that!"

"Of course not," replied Laura quickly. "But what can we tell the others? How did you happen to know? They will wonder."

"Just as I said, I saw it. It had no sooner been mentioned than I saw where it was. I didn't try to see it. It just happened."

Elliot sank down wearily on the window seat, his fists clenched on his knees. Laura sat beside him. Elliot's gift seemed more and more remarkable.

"That's all you saw. Where it was?"

Elliot nodded. "I'd give anything to know how it got there. They must all be thinking terrible things about me."

"Well, they must know you didn't take the locket and put it there. When could you have done it? You all arrived together and were with each other the entire time before dinner," said Laura.

Elliot shook his head.

"That isn't the way it was, though. I came over first, you see. I rode your pony and returned it to the stables. I was here some time before the others arrived. So you see, they could suspect me. No one will believe I saw it in my mind. Oh, why did I say that?"

"Because it was the truth," said Laura loyally. "I know it's the truth. There must be some way to prove it. Perhaps if we could determine when the locket was taken, then—"

Laura broke off abruptly.

"I think I know when it happened," she cried excitedly and told him about the mysteriously closing door. She recalled for him the scene in the schoolroom, when she had thought she had seen Alexandra going into her room, although it turned out not to be Alexandra at all, for she was sitting before the fire.

"Someone most definitely was in Alexandra's room before dinner," she cried triumphantly.

Elliot did not seem to think this was particularly enlightening or encouraging.

"We still don't know who it was or why," he said. "It might have been a maid, after all. Oh, it's just no good. Not any of it. I am a danger to myself, and, what is more, I probably won't be able to help Peters either. You should have let me stay in my room. It was the only sensible thing to do."

Laura had always been a cheerful, optimistic person. To see Elliot give in to despair was, in her eyes, the worst kind of weakness. It made her simply furious to think that anyone would be so easily defeated. She could see only merit in fighting back.

She rose and stood looking down angrily at Elliot.

"Very well, if that is the way you feel, that is what you should do. Go back to your house. Shut yourself up in your room. Do not expect me to feel sorry for you."

Before Elliot could reply, Laura left the room and hurried upstairs.

There she threw herself upon her bed and wept. They were tears of anger and frustration, and at length they exhausted her. She undressed at last and fell into a troubled sleep.

Long before dawn, she awoke with the uncanny sensation that she was not alone in the room. Her first impulse was to call out and ask who was there, but she stifled it.

Cautiously she sat up and peered through an opening in her bed curtain. What she saw frightened her into si-

lence. She hardly dared breathe. In the far corner of her room, near the dressing table, was a woman. She was a ghostly stooped figure with a shawl over her head that completely covered the upper part of her body. All around the woman was a weird, flickering glow that made it possible for Laura to see dimly. The figure was hardly more than a shadow in the darkness. Who could she be? What was she? The unearthly glow made her seem unreal and very like a phantom.

Laura's heart pounded wildly with fright. She felt as though she could not move. But she must! She must call out for Miss Haversmith or one of the servants. She must!

Laura was about to try, when a high sharp sound pierced the stillness outside. She glanced nervously in the direction of the sound, but saw only the blank, vacant face of the open window. When she looked back into the room, the figure had vanished as though it had never been.

Laura had often heard stories the servants told of the ghosts of Covington Castle. She had believed none of them, for she had never herself seen a ghost. Had she seen one now? The apparition had disappeared so quickly, it was almost possible to believe it had not been human.

Laura shook her head. She was ashamed of her thoughts. Quickly she got out of bed and lighted a candle. She could not control her trembling. Nonetheless, she ventured to the dressing table and began to examine it.

Something was not quite right. Laura stared at the tabletop. There in the very center was a drop of wax. Gingerly she touched it with the tip of her finger. It was still hot. Then she caught her breath. The miniature of her father was gone! Only this afternoon it had stood there in its small, gilt frame.

First Alexandra's locket, and now her own miniature.

Someone had gone to a great deal of trouble to obtain a likeness of her father. Why?

That such devious efforts would not be made for any friendly purpose, Laura was sure. She was overwhelmed with fear for her father's safety.

Three men had vanished from Tonbridge Wells, and everyone had abandoned hope of ever seeing them again. Elliot had already received warning concerning a fourth. What if Father were meant to be the fifth?

Laura wished now she had not been so hasty in judging Elliot's behavior that evening. How easy it was to feel despair when you were faced with what appeared to be unsolvable problems.

She must contact Elliot and beg his forgiveness. No matter what Miss Haversmith said about confining her to her room, she would see him. She would convince Elliot that they could prevent disaster. He must agree now, for her father's sake.

7

Lost in the Maze

Laura was awakened by Martha the next morning.

"Miss Haversmith says you are to ride today, even though you are to keep to your room after lessons. She says daily exercise cannot be neglected."

For a moment Laura stared blankly at the cheerful girl. Had last night's ghostly visit been but a dream? It certainly seemed so now. Martha laid out Laura's riding things and appeared to be trying to hide a smile.

"I suspect Miss Haversmith never climbed a tree in her life, miss," she said and giggled outright at the thought.

Laura was too confused and upset to explain that Miss Haversmith had not discovered that particular misdemeanor as yet. The second that Martha left, Laura hurried to examine her dressing table. The miniature was indeed missing. She at once became as frightened as she had been the night before. The apparition had been no dream. Someone had stolen her father's portrait. For what purpose? Laura's resolve to speak to Elliot was stronger than ever.

Laura and Alexandra set off from the stables with Miss

Haversmith, as usual, in the mists of early morning.

"Oh, how uncommonly hot it is for early June!" complained Alexandra. "Let us ride beside the sea. At least there might be a cooling breeze."

Laura was disappointed.

"I thought we might go past the manor and on to Witch's Cottage," she said casually. That would give them the best chance of accidentally coming across Elliot, but Laura supposed Miss Haversmith would never agree. She was wrong.

"I don't think it wise to ride in the direction of the sea, Alexandra," the governess told them gravely. "It is in that very area that so many of our young men have vanished. No, Witch's Cottage is best for today."

Miss Haversmith's word was law, and Alexandra could do nothing but give in. They rode along in silence, first Miss Haversmith, then Alexandra, and last of all Laura. Since conversation was not required of her, Laura had ample time to ponder a plan to see Elliot.

Almost at once she thought of the maze in the side garden. The manor was well known for its maze. Years ago, perhaps before Lady Simpson-Favorite had even been born, the gardeners had designed the maze by cutting hedges to form walls.

Father said the maze was very like the one at Hampton Court near London. Within the walls was an intricate series of paths that led and misled anyone who entered the maze. Laura knew that one might easily become lost, traveling down one path after another only to find a blind alley. Still, she felt sure that if she did not go in too far, she would be able to get out quickly enough.

As they approached the magnificent wrought-iron gates that, when closed, displayed the Simpson-Favorite coat of arms in the center, Laura saw her opportunity. The gates were open.

She slowed her pony until she was riding well behind the others. Suddenly, without warning, she bolted on through the gates. She knew that Miss Haversmith would follow eventually, but Laura hoped to reach the maze beyond the west gardens and hide there before anyone saw her. She did not like to deceive her governess, but this time she thought it was necessary.

It took a few moments for Miss Haversmith to believe her charge's astonishing behavior. This was all Laura needed. She raced along the wide carriageway until she came to an opening in the high, well-shaped yew hedges. Now she was hidden from view and made straightaway for the gardens and the maze.

Laura was not so familiar with the maze as she might have been had there been children living at the manor. Had that been the case, she might have played here often and come to know the secret of the paths that led in and out and those which merely teased one on to nowhere.

There were very few occasions when Laura had visited the maze herself, and those had been in company with her father. Nevertheless, the northeast entrance was not difficult for her to find. She rode on a way, following the twistings and turnings created by the carefully clipped hedges, and then dismounted, calming her pony with soft words.

Now that she was there, she had no idea what to do next. She was not in the least certain of the way out, and how was she to contact Elliot?

The maze was quite extensive, so she might hide there for hours without being discovered. No doubt Miss Haversmith would expect her to go directly to the house. Laura was safe for the moment.

She walked slowly along, leading her pony, until she saw a white stone bench. There she sat down to rest. When she looked up, all she could see were narrow walls of green hedges and the hazy morning sky above. There was no sound from outside. She decided to wait half an hour before venturing out. But how could she judge the time? When the mists lifted entirely and the sky appeared to be blue again, she decided, she would go in search of Elliot.

Her pony was quite content to bend his head and chomp the longer tufts of grass that grew at the edge of the path. Laura wondered if she ought to explore the maze further. It might be important to discover another way out in the event that someone came searching for her. What if Mr. Tonner or his sister decided to join in the search? They might very quickly think of the maze, for they had lived there as children.

The thought had no sooner entered Laura's mind than she heard voices near at hand.

"I can't think what has got into the child. Something must have affected her mind. She has never run away before. Never!"

Miss Haversmith's firm, clear tones were colored with annoyance, as well as anxiety.

"Pray, do not disturb yourself, my dear. Children love to play games. I daresay little Laura is hiding. We shall certainly find her in a matter of minutes. Come, follow me," said Mr. Tonner.

Laura leaped to her feet. She would almost certainly be discovered if she did not move quickly. If she were found, she would lose all hope of seeing Elliot, and her daring act of disobedience would have been all for nothing. But which way should she go? Reluctantly she decided to leave her pony behind. She could hide better alone.

"I am distressed to be forced to disturb you for such foolishness, Mr. Tonner." Miss Haversmith's voice was dangerously close. "This is certainly not a fortuitous way to begin the day."

"Any reason that brings me the pleasure of your company seems most fortuitous to me, my dear Miss Haversmith," replied Mr. Tonner.

Laura turned quickly to the right. Only the width of a hedge seemed to separate them. She rushed down a narrow lane only to find herself up against a blank, a dead end. She turned and hurried back the way she had come.

"Don't worry so, my dear," Laura heard Mr. Tonner saying. "It grieves me to see such a look in your lovely eyes. Come, let us have a smile. There, that is so much better."

Laura found herself back where she had started. Her pony was still cropping grass beside the stone bench. Laura was nearly frantic. Charming and solicitous as Mr. Tonner might sound now, she had the feeling his mood could change in an instant. She did not want to be found by him. Miss Haversmith's anger would be far easier to face.

The voices were so close, Laura was certain she must run headlong into her pursuers. Still, the turn to the right had led nowhere. She walked back the way she had entered the maze and came to a place where she might turn either right or left. Left, she decided this time. Though that seemed the direction of the voices, Laura followed along a path leading at the end to another right turn, and the voices faded until she could hear them no more.

With a sigh of relief, she realized she had eluded Miss Haversmith and Mr. Tonner. Then she gasped in surprise and fear. She had thought she had nothing to fear from anything in the maze other than her governess and Elliot's uncle. And yet suddenly she found herself confronted by a creature whose appearance terrified her. It was a figure part human, part goat, with the most gruesome eyes and pointed ears she had ever seen. It loomed at the end of the path. There seemed no escape. Laura tried not to scream and clasped her hands to her mouth, but a cry did escape. Who or what was this devilish creature?

"Hush, Laura! It's only a statue—a satyr! They'll hear you!"

Laura whirled about, nearly fainting from fright and relief at the same time.

"Oh, Elliot! Thank goodness I've found you," she whispered. "Whatever are you doing here?"

"Looking for you, of course. Hurry! They are not far away."

"Looking for me? But how did you know where to look?" she asked and realized immediately the foolishness of such a question. Would she ever get used to the fact that Elliot knew things without being told?

Elliot's dark hair was tousled, and he appeared to have dressed in a hurry, for some of his shirt buttons were still undone. He reached for Laura's arm and led her rapidly and rather unceremoniously through a series of paths until at last they found themselves outside the maze where two horses were saddled and waiting.

Laura noticed that Elliot had seemed to feel his way through the maze by running his hand along the left wall.

"The trick is never make a turn that requires you to lift that hand," he explained. "I am quite familiar with mazes. Now, follow me."

He helped Laura mount one of the horses. The fine animal was much bigger than her own pony, and the stirrups needed adjusting. This Elliot did hurriedly. In no time at all they were on their way.

They left the manor by jumping the hedges of the north gardens and, to Laura's surprise, began to ride east in the direction of the common meadow and the sea.

Laura longed to stop and take the time to apologize for her behavior of the evening before. She was beginning to feel the pangs of hunger too, now that the danger of being discovered was past. After all, she had had no breakfast. She urged her horse forward and drew up beside Elliot as they crossed the road.

"Don't worry," he said before she could speak. "I've brought along something to eat, and you must not blame yourself about last night. I quite understand. I was entirely wrong."

Laura began to wonder if Elliot often knew what was in other people's minds. If so, it would be most disconcerting. Imagine having to guard one's very thoughts every time he was about!

Laura was only mildly alarmed to be riding through the common meadow behind Covington Castle. It was, after all, only grown men who had vanished here so mysteriously. Surely Elliot would know if there was any danger. But when Elliot allowed their horses to wade right through the Nailbourne itself and then dash for the willows that encircled the hidden cove, she grew anxious. They drew up before the old windmill.

"Father said the mill was dangerous, Elliot." Laura felt she must remind him.

"Yes, but it is a good place to hide. No one will think to look for us here. No villagers will bring their cattle to the meadow today. And we will be careful."

Elliot dismounted and helped Laura down. He tied the horses to a convenient willow branch and then examined the steps that led to the mill. He tested them carefully and pronounced them safe.

"We can sit here at least and enjoy our breakfast," he said. He carried from his saddlebag a package of biscuits, jam, and a whole cheese.

"Nothing to drink, I'm afraid," he admitted. "I couldn't think how to carry any tea. But perhaps the waters of the Nailbourne—" he began.

"Oh, no!" Laura was shocked, but Elliot only laughed.

"It's fresh, spring water. Pure as snow. Your father said so. You heard him yourself."

"Oh, Elliot! It's Father whom I must speak to you about," said Laura.

Before she would even taste the biscuits, she told him everything about what she had seen the night before and about the missing miniature.

"What can it all mean?" she asked. "I can't but think that Father is in some sort of danger. Someone has gone to great difficulty to get a likeness of him."

Elliot was silent. His dark eyes were sad. "I don't know," he said at last. "I have not been able to learn more about that strange fire and explosion either. I've tried time and time again. There has been nothing until I woke and saw you running in the maze this morning."

"You saw me?"

"Yes, in my mind. Unexpectedly, like the locket, you know."

He smiled wryly. "No one believed that. Your mother and sister must think me quite strange. Even Aunt Madelaine is alarmed."

"No one accused you of anything?"

"Surprisingly enough, no one mentioned the locket to me afterward. It was returned, and the circumstances of its being missing were all too shameful, I expect. I'm sure it shan't be forgotten altogether. Last night I learned Uncle George has no immediate plans for leaving Tonbridge Wells. He won't forget. Not only that, he and Aunt Georgina keep insisting that Aunt Madelaine is not well and needs their help."

"Is Lady Simpson-Favorite really ill?" asked Laura.

"I hardly think so," replied Elliot. He looked down, noticed that his cuffs were undone, and began to remedy the matter.

"I don't like the way they behave around her. She is old and weak, it is true. But to suggest that she is ill!" He shook his head. "It is almost too much for her. She has promised to remain in her bed all day today resting. I tell you I don't like it at all."

Elliot looked up at Laura, who was sitting a step above him, her biscuits still untouched.

"Here, aren't you going to eat at all? You must be famished. Try some jam."

He passed the small silver container to her, and Laura began to eat. The early-morning ride and all the excitement had made her hungry. She ate four biscuits and was satisfied.

The long, drooping branches of the willows circled the cove and formed a perfect hiding place. The surface of the water, which was usually still, seemed to ripple and move slowly. The water level was higher than Laura remembered it.

"Have you no idea who it was who came and took the miniature last night?" asked Elliot.

"None," said Laura, "except that it seemed to be a woman, a ghostly woman."

"Perhaps that was simply what you were meant to think."

Elliot closed his eyes.

"If only I could feel something, see something!" He sighed. "Nothing!"

Laura got to her feet. She could not sit still a minute longer.

"Let us ride to the village. Perhaps if you actually saw that—that building. You said it was very like a church. If we found it, wouldn't that help?"

"It might."

"Do try, Elliot," begged Laura. "For Father's sake you must try."

The Riderless Horse

The children were just leaving the shelter of the willows when the sounds of an approaching horse reached them. Elliot signaled Laura to retreat, and they watched, hidden by the screen of low-hanging branches, as a riderless white horse trotted across the meadow.

"We've seen him before," whispered Laura. "Yesterday from the tree in the walled garden, remember? But where is the rider?"

Elliot did not reply. He was watching the horse, which had slowed to a walk and seemed to be wandering about aimlessly. Someone had saddled him and then thrown the reins carelessly across his neck. The reins slid to the ground as the magnificent animal bent his head to drink from the waters of the Nailbourne.

It gave Laura an eerie sensation to watch the lonely creature.

"You do remember, don't you, Elliot?" she asked, more to savor the reassuring sound of a human voice than from a desire for information. Of course they had both seen the horse.

But Elliot did not seem to hear. He was staring at what appeared to be nothing, as Laura had seen him stare before.

"Elliot, is anything wrong?" she asked fearfully.

Elliot was pale, and there were tiny beads of perspiration on his forehead.

"No— No—" he faltered. "Why should anything be wrong?"

Laura was surprised. Was Elliot being honest with her?

"I thought perhaps you had seen something," she suggested gently.

Elliot denied this. "There was nothing."

He led his horse away from the willows and mounted him.

"Can you manage, yourself?" he asked, glancing back at her and then quickly away.

Laura grasped her horse's mane and, with an effort, pulled herself into the saddle. She wanted to look into Elliot's eyes to see if what she suspected was true. He must have seen something, something so awful he did not want her to know about it. Did it have to do with Father?

"Wait!" she cried, as he galloped off toward Tonbridge Wells. But he refused to slow down or even to look at her.

He is afraid, thought Laura. He is afraid I shall see the truth in his eyes.

Elliot cut across the meadow and led the way through a grove of elms before they reached the road. Laura raced after him. As they approached the first cottages, he finally stopped and looked about.

"Look!" he cried. "See the cottages. Every one is shuttered."

"Against the heat of the day no doubt," said Laura reasonably. This was not what she wanted to hear. "Elliot, please. You saw something just now. What was it?"

The line of Elliot's jaw was stubbornly set. He would not look her straight in the face.

"I saw nothing," he insisted. "Why do you keep asking?"

This denial only worried Laura all the more. But if Elliot refused to speak, what could she do?

"Doesn't it seem strange to you that no one is about?" he asked, frowning.

"They have chores," replied Laura without really thinking about it.

Elliot was used to city life where the streets were never empty. "The villagers work hard. You cannot expect them to stand about idly gossiping," she added rather impatiently.

"But surely someone should be about. There is not even a child."

Laura followed his gaze down the narrow dirt road and saw that he was quite right. The village of Tonbridge Wells looked deserted. Laura finally realized the significance of the situation. It was odd, as if everyone in the entire village simply had disappeared. The thought was frightening.

"Well, the place can't really be deserted," she said slowly. "Where would everyone go, and why?"

"Precisely," said Elliot.

"I think we are taking too much for granted," said Laura. She had just spied the cottage of the Widow Bombray. "There is a way to find out for certain."

She led Elliot to the widow's cottage, where she dismounted and rapped on the stout, wooden door.

"I visited here only recently. This is the home of the widow who lost a son to the Nailbourne and a husband as well, as I told you. She will certainly be able to tell us, should anything be really wrong."

Although Laura rapped repeatedly, and Elliot joined her in her efforts, no one answered.

"It's useless," said Elliot. "It must be as we thought. Everyone is gone."

Laura refused to accept this conclusion.

"Mrs. Bombray! Mrs. Bombray!" she called in a loud voice. "It is I, Laura Covington, and Elliot Simpson-Favorite! Do please let us in. We wish only to speak with you."

There was a shuffling sound from within, and heavy bolts were released. The door opened ever so slightly, and the children saw Mrs. Bombray's frightened eyes gazing at them in wonder.

"The Lord bless you!" she exclaimed, opening the door just enough to let the children inside. "What are you doing hereabouts, you poor dears?"

Laura found it difficult for her eyes to adjust to the dim light of the interior. Nevertheless, it was obvious that the widow was in a state of extreme distress. She quickly rebolted the door.

"We were out riding, Mrs. Bombray," explained Laura, after politely presenting Elliot, "and we noticed the village was unaccountably quiet. Is anything wrong?"

"Wrong! Oh, Lord love you, miss. Nothing in the world is right!"

Mrs. Bombray paused to wipe her eyes with the hem of her apron. "Last night five more of our best men disappeared. There was some as went to the vicar for advice.

He bid them pray to the dear Lord to remove the curse of the Nailbourne from Tonbridge Wells. And he advised us all to stay at home. You'll find no one abroad in Tonbridge Wells today."

"Five more villagers!" exclaimed Elliot. "How did this happen?"

"No one knows, but sometime in the late evening, when the mists began to close in, they were taken," replied the widow, her voice breaking with emotion. "They were not in their beds this morning. May the dear Lord have pity on us all!" She bowed her head.

"Yes," said Laura. She did not know what else to say.

Laura and Elliot lingered only minutes longer and then left, followed by the anxious pleas of the widow to seek shelter at once or to accept her hospitality.

Elliot began to travel back along the road they had come.

"We must get you to safety at once," he told Laura.

"I?" asked Laura. "I? I am in no danger. It is only men who disappear," she reminded him. "We can't go back now. We must find the building you saw. St. John's Church is not far from here. We must proceed there at once."

"But under the circumstances—" Elliot hesitated and was lost. Laura simply rode away from him toward the center of the village. He was forced to follow.

The cottages here were closer together, their heavy thatched roofs reaching nearly to the ground. All windows were closed and tightly shuttered. The horses' hoofbeats were the only sound that disturbed the deep quiet of the morning.

Even the Black Swan Inn appeared to be closed, although as she passed by, Laura imagined she heard voices and even laughter from within. But the fancy left her as they rounded a bend in the road and found themselves facing the village green with the church and the vicarage on the far side.

"There it is. That is St. John's Church. It does have quite a spire. Is it anything at all like the building you saw?" asked Laura, searching her friend's face anxiously for the least sign of recognition.

Elliot's disappointment was obvious. "Oh," he cried. "This is nothing like it. Nothing like it at all. Is this the only building you can think of? Are there no other perpendicular structures about?"

"This is all I can think of," replied Laura unhappily. "Beyond the green are only more cottages and then nothing but the road to Dover."

"I had *so* hoped it might be the church," said Elliot in despair. "We must find it. We must! Now more than ever!"

Elliot squeezed his eyes tightly shut in exasperation. "Think, Laura, think!" he begged.

"I am thinking. Really, I am."

Laura had dismounted rather ungracefully, owing to the height of her horse. She led him into the shade of the large oak that grew in the village square.

"It's getting late, Elliot," she said. "I dare not stay away too much longer. Why did you think the building was a church to begin with?"

Elliot joined her on the stone bench beneath the tree.

"It was the spire, I expect. There was a spire."

Laura sighed. The only spire in Tonbridge Wells was atop St. John's. "Are you quite sure, Elliot?"

"Quite," said Elliot. "We must find it. You said my

strange gift might be used to help others. I cannot bear to know of such suffering and be helpless! What can I do? What can I do?"

Laura could see that he had gone quite pale, and she meant to encourage him as best she could.

"We'll find it, Elliot. Together we shall do it," she said, sounding much more confident than she felt. "But you must share what you have seen with me. How else can I help?"

She paused to add weight to her words, then went on in a quiet voice. "Whom did you see astride the white horse? Tell me the truth, Elliot. Was it my father?"

Elliot sat up slowly and gazed sadly at Laura.

"All right," he said at last. "Yes, it was your father."

"Oh, dear," cried Laura miserably.

"I didn't want you to know. I didn't want you to worry," said Elliot.

Laura choked back a sob. "What do you think it means? Perhaps Father should be warned not to mount the horse."

She stood up quickly, anxious for action. "Perhaps he is home already, or perhaps a message can be sent."

Elliot made no move to go.

"It's too late for that. He has already ridden the horse," he said in a dismal tone. "It was probably he whom we saw in the meadow only yesterday."

Laura felt herself grow cold with apprehension, but she felt she could not accept this. "That is not possible. Father has not been here in nearly a week," she cried. "He has been in London. You are mistaken. You must be!"

Even as she spoke, Laura knew that Elliot was not mistaken. She stood gripping the reins of her horse so tightly her small hands ached with the pressure. She would never give way to tears! But where was Father? What had happened to him? Surely he could not be—

"Elliot, you must tell me," she cried, dropping the reins and grasping one of his hands in both of hers. "Is my father— That is, surely he cannot be dead."

The sound of the word horrified her, but she had to know.

Elliot spoke slowly. "I feel that he is not. But understand, it is only something I feel."

The relief that flooded Laura's heart was overwhelming. She pressed Elliot's hands in gratitude. So great was her respect for his unusual gift that his assurance that there was still hope for her father was all she needed.

"Thank you, dear Elliot. I am certain that we shall find him."

Elliot was by no means as confident, but he hid his misgivings admirably.

Laura positioned her horse before the bench and climbed upon it to mount him.

"We shall begin by interviewing Mother," she told Elliot. "Perhaps Father's business did not take him to London after all. Perhaps he confided in her. I am sure when you have told her what you have seen, she will confide in us."

Elliot found such a prospect quite distressing.

"I hardly think so, Laura," he protested. "Only remember the skepticism with which everyone greeted the information I let fall about Alexandra's locket last evening. It does not seem to me that Lady Caroline would regard seriously anything I had to say."

But Laura was not listening. She was already galloping ahead. So swiftly did the two of them ride that this time Laura was not even aware of the rather loud voices raised behind the shuttered windows of Black Swan Inn.

As the gates of Covington Castle arose in the distance, Laura reined in her horse. She was not certain of the best way to approach her home. If Miss Haversmith discovered them before they were able to see Mother, an interview might be difficult to achieve.

"I think, Elliot, we should make our entrance through one of the gardens. There would be less chance of being seen," Laura suggested.

And so they did, careful not to trod upon the beautifully tended beds of flowers that lined the walks. They dismounted near the garden house and left their horses there. Quickly they made their way toward the broad terraces of Covington Castle.

Laura would have led Elliot to one of the stone staircases, but the sound of voices on the terrace caused her to stop. She and Elliot stood completely concealed below and listened.

"Laura is an impulsive child, but such disobedience simply astounds me. What can have got into her?" said Lady Covington.

"I feel I must apologize for my nephew."

Laura recognized Mr. Tonner's voice. "It is he who is to blame, I am sure. It must be that he has filled her head with his own mad tales. I assure you, my dear Lady Caroline, that I shall take steps at once to have him sent away and confined for his own good as well as that of others. We must face facts. He is certainly mad and must be cared for accordingly."

Horrified, Laura turned to Elliot, but he held a silencing finger to his lips and motioned her to press closer to the stone wall to avoid any danger of being seen.

"It was a sad day, Lady Caroline, when that poor,

demented boy came to stay with my aunt. Lady Simpson-Favorite is in delicate health, and I can tell you that Elliot's shocking behavior has considerably weakened her. I am afraid she has taken to her bed."

"I am so sorry," said Laura's mother. "You must tell her for me that the very moment I know my daughter is safe, I shall send a message. There must be something I can do."

"Lady Caroline, you are most kind—" began Mr. Tonner, but he was interrupted by Miss Haversmith's agitated tones.

"The gardeners report two horses from the Simpson-Favorite stables on the grounds. The children cannot be far away," she announced.

Hardly had she spoken than Laura grasped Elliot's arm and led him around to a partially concealed door on the far side of the terrace. Quietly they slipped inside to the safety of Lord Covington's wine cellar.

There was a small lamp burning near the stairs at the far end of the neat rows of bottles, which were carefully placed on their sides and meticulously labeled in their wooden racks.

"I don't think," said Elliot after a moment, "that it would be wise for me to speak to your mother at this particular time."

"Nor would it be wise to return to the manor. You must stay here, Elliot. There are parts of the castle no one ever visits. The turrets, for instance. You could be safe there until we know how to proceed."

Laura was terribly grieved for Elliot's dreadful predicament. She knew he had neither liked nor trusted his uncle from the beginning. But she had never expected Mr. Tonner to be so—so evil. The very idea of sending Elliot away

94

to some madman's asylum proved that Mr. Tonner was anxious to be rid of his nephew once and for all.

"Heaven knows what he has done to poor Aunt Madelaine!" whispered Elliot, as though they had been thinking the same thoughts. "You must find out, Laura."

"I will, as soon as possible."

Laura's mind had been working rapidly, planning how best to conceal Elliot and make her own entrance.

"Elliot, do you think you could find the southwest turret alone? There is a small room at the top. No one ever goes there. The servants think it is haunted. It would be a matter of climbing these stairs that lead to the servants' quarters, then slipping through to the back stairs. There is a circular stairway from the second-floor gallery to the turret. You can't miss it. There are two huge Grecian urns on either side of the door to the stairs."

"I'll find it," said Elliot. "What will you do?"

"Go back to the garden and enter through the terrace. I shall come to you as soon as I can," she promised.

Laura had no way of knowing when that might be. She felt she would certainly be punished for her disobedience. She was not prepared for forgiveness.

A Daring Plan

"Oh, my darling child!" exclaimed Lady Covington, when Laura suddenly appeared at the top of the terrace steps. Her mother hurried forward and gathered Laura into her arms, covering her with kisses.

Laura clung to her mother while warily observing the effect of her homecoming upon Mr. Tonner and Miss Haversmith.

"Darling Laura!" her mother went on. "We have been so worried. Do you know how worried we have been? Whatever possessed you to run off like that? Your governess and I have been frantic, thinking all sorts of dreadful things. Why did you do it? Where have you been?"

Lady Covington paused for breath, but not long enough for an answer. "When Mr. Tonner found your pony in the maze and no sign of you— Well, after all that has been happening in Tonbridge Wells, you must know we were terrified."

Lady Caroline returned to her chair, still holding Laura about the waist and looking lovingly into her eyes.

Laura was surprised and rather pleased by her mother's

demonstrative behavior. It would be pleasant if Mother would show affection more often. Laura leaned forward now and kissed her mother's cheek.

"I never meant to worry you, Mama."

Laura knew that she must give some sort of explanation for her behavior without involving Elliot too much, and she soon hit upon a plan.

"But I did mean to worry Miss Haversmith!" she announced.

Until this very moment Miss Haversmith had been standing with her hands primly clasped before her. At Laura's astonishing words, the governess gasped.

Lady Covington recovered quickly from the initial shock of this confession. "Laura, this is most unlike you," she admonished gently. "Surely you can see how dreadfully cruel that was. Whatever could have prompted you to do such a thing?"

"Was it by some chance suggested by my unfortunate nephew?" asked Mr. Tonner.

His lips were smiling, but Laura was very much aware of his unsmiling eyes. "Elliot seems to have a way of, shall we say, influencing others?"

"No, Mr. Tonner, it was all my own idea. Miss Haversmith meant to punish me for having neglected to come when required yesterday afternoon. I suppose I resented the idea and dashed off into the maze to tease her," Laura improvised smoothly.

She raised her eyes to meet those of her governess. "I never meant to cause you any real pain," she added and was surprised to note that Miss Haversmith's eyes seemed unnaturally bright with unshed tears.

Why, she does care, thought Laura. I have hurt her.

"Please, Miss Haversmith, I truly am sorry now. Of

course I deserved to be punished," added Laura with deep sincerity. "Can you forgive me?"

Miss Haversmith's severe expression softened. "We are all given to impulse now and then," she conceded. "But you left the maze and your pony. Where did you go?"

"Riding with Elliot. I met him in the maze," said Laura, as though that were the most natural thing in the world. "We rode into Tonbridge Wells. You know, he hasn't had much opportunity to see the village since he has been here."

She turned to her mother. "Did you know that five more men have vanished? All the houses are shuttered and barred. No one is about for fear of being taken. Can't something be done?"

"Yes, it is dreadful," said Lady Covington, shaking her head sadly. "I had word from the vicar only this morning."

Mr. Tonner seemed disinclined to discuss the problems of the villagers. He rose and prepared to leave.

"Well, now that dear Laura has returned safely, I must go to Aunt Madelaine. Tell me, child, where do you think young Elliot is now?" he asked carefully.

Laura raised wide, innocent eyes to his.

"Why, Mr. Tonner, I should imagine he would be at home. No doubt he wants his luncheon. It must be well past time."

As she spoke Laura was alarmed to recall that the two horses from the Simpson-Favorite stables had been discovered in the Covington gardens. She could think of no way to explain that and decided not to try. So many young men had simply vanished. Why not Elliot too? One could think he had the best intentions of returning to the manor and then had been taken.

Laura fervently hoped that Elliot had by now reached the safety of the southwest turret. After a moment of thoughtful silence, Mr. Tonner moved to go. Evidently he had decided to seek Elliot at home.

"Miss Haversmith, do please see Mr. Tonner to his carriage. I find I am quite exhausted," said Lady Caroline, raising a limp hand to her forehead. "I hope you will excuse me, sir?"

"Of course," said Mr. Tonner, bowing, and he left with Miss Haversmith on his arm.

"You should certainly rest, Mother," said Laura.

"I shall," promised Lady Covington.

Laura herself hurried upstairs, hoping to find Elliot before luncheon was served. Unfortunately, she found instead that her governess had left instructions for Laura to wait in the schoolroom.

When Miss Haversmith arrived, she regarded Laura with disapproval.

"We have wasted the entire morning, thanks to you, young miss. Therefore, we shall have our luncheon and begin our lessons immediately thereafter. Be so good as to change your clothes at once."

Laura thought of Elliot shut up in the turret room awaiting her. He must be both anxious and hungry. She knew she must find some way to see him and bring food. That would have to wait, perhaps hours now. She could not risk seeking the turret room at this time. She resigned herself to an afternoon of anxiety.

Not until late afternoon, following a dreary tea during which Miss Haversmith insisted they speak nothing but French as part of that day's lessons, did Laura manage to slip away. She was truly grateful for Miss Haversmith's softened attitude. There was to be no punishment after all.

The problem of supplying food for Elliot was easily surmounted. Laura sent Martha down to bring her a second tea.

"I never get enough to eat when I am obliged to request everything in French," Laura explained. "I have such difficulty remembering the words for everything that cakes and sandwiches are all gone before I can ask for them."

Martha giggled. "She wouldn't know what a real appetite is, miss," said the girl, referring to Miss Haversmith. "Too dignified to eat, she is. Hardly touches her breakfast. You wait, miss. I'll bring you something."

After Miss Haversmith and Alexandra retired to their rooms, Laura, carrying the heavy tray Martha had brought, made her way through empty halls to the gallery and the turret stairs.

A narrow, circular staircase led to one of the highest rooms in the castle. This was concealed behind a heavy door that Laura found difficult to open. She was beginning to think it had in some way become locked. But it gave way finally, after she had placed the tray upon one of the urns beside the door and pulled with both hands. Elliot met her on the dusty stairs, a lighted taper in his hand.

"I thought you'd never come," he said. "Once or twice I almost came down to look for you. What has been happening? Have you had news of Aunt Madelaine?"

He led the way to the round tower room where they were forced to sit on the wooden floor, for there were no furnishings. The pale light of the taper Elliot had found in the wall did little to dispel the gloomy shadows. The only other light came from rays of late afternoon sun which found their way through the long, narrow slits in the stone walls.

"I am sorry, Elliot. I came as soon as I safely could. Here, eat the cheese dish at once while it's hot."

She removed silver covers, and Elliot ate with such appetite as would have warmed the heart of Lady Covington's excellent cook. All the while Laura told him of her interview with her mother and Mr. Tonner.

"I believe he does mean to confine you somewhere, Elliot. He is looking for you. He made a point of calling you his 'unfortunate nephew.' He is convinced you are mad."

"He is convinced," said Elliot, touching his lips with the napkin, "that by ridding himself of me and Aunt Madelaine, he will quickly gain control of the Simpson-Favorite fortune. He is a ruthless man."

Laura understood only too well how Mr. Tonner planned to rid himself of Elliot. "But Lady Simpson-Favorite has never been thought to be mad," she said. "How does he plan to rid himself of your great-aunt?"

"I think a sudden, fatal illness would suffice, don't you?" asked Elliot.

"Elliot! He wouldn't—He could not think of harming her!"

"I am afraid he could," said Elliot grimly. His dark eyes had grown darker with anger.

"Do you know that?" asked Laura.

"If you mean have I foreseen anything, no. I have not seen Aunt Madelaine since last evening. At that time there was no hint, but I have a strong feeling that those are Uncle George's plans, or something like them. There," he said, throwing down his napkin and sighing, "I feel so much better."

Then he leaned toward Laura and spoke earnestly.

"I have had ample time to think. I feel the best solution

for Aunt Madelaine is to lure her away from the manor. If she should come here, for instance, she would be safe."

"Come here? But how can we arrange it?"

"Suppose she were to receive an urgent message from your mother."

"But if Mr. Tonner's intentions are as you suspect, would he not intercept the message, or discourage her from coming?"

"Yes, but only suppose you brought the message yourself," said Elliot.

"Of course I am quite willing to do anything you suggest, Elliot. But surely Mr. Tonner or his sister would not allow me to see your aunt."

"Quite so! However, I plan to engage their attentions away from the house. Tell me, Laura," said Elliot, standing up. "Your governess is a small woman. I am nearly as tall as she, am I not?"

Laura looked critically at Elliot, trying to recollect Miss Haversmith's height. "Yes, I think so."

"And were I to wear her cloak, perhaps from a distance I might be taken for her, do you think?"

Laura nodded, too surprised to comment on such a suggestion.

"Then I shall require Miss Haversmith's cloak, pen and ink, some of her notepaper, and perhaps a sample of her writing. Can you manage all that within the hour?"

Laura simply stared.

"I know it is a good deal to ask, and it might seem that I am not concentrating my attention on finding your father. But you know, I believe Uncle George somehow holds the key to your father's whereabouts."

"Oh," cried Laura, her eyes bright with hope. She

picked up the tea tray. "Nothing shall prevent me from fulfilling your requests, Elliot."

Miss Haversmith's cloak was easier to find than Laura expected. There it was, hanging on the inside of the bedroom door, and no one at all around to see Laura take it. Miss Haversmith's room was quiet. A slight breeze lifted the curtains at the window. Other than that there was no movement, no sound at all. It was strange to be in this room uninvited. Laura looked about her at the neatly covered bed, the wardrobe, and the three-drawer dresser with only a small looking glass above it. There was no dressing table. Everything was plain and orderly like Miss Haversmith herself.

Plain, thought Laura. Was Miss Haversmith entirely plain? She had been actually pretty the night the Tonners had dined here. Where, she wondered, was the scarlet dress now? It was nowhere in evidence. How difficult it was to know what people were really like! For instance, who would have suspected that Laura would be here now, or that she would take anything that did not belong to her? And yet she was doing just that.

With only a slight qualm, Laura took two sheets of notepaper, as well as an envelope, from the desk. At any time she expected Miss Haversmith to burst in upon her and cry "thief." But Laura found she had the courage of desperation and did all that she had to do.

The matter of handwriting gave her some difficulty until she thought of her own copybook. Miss Haversmith often wrote lengthy comments on Laura's work. There were many examples of her governess' handwriting in the book. Half an hour later she returned to Elliot with everything.

"Splendid," Elliot complimented her. "And this writing should not be difficult to imitate."

Swiftly he composed a note requesting Mr. Tonner and his sister to meet Miss Haversmith in the maze "on a matter of utmost urgency."

"Why the maze?" asked Laura.

"Why not the maze?" asked Elliot. "What better place for an impostor to hide? And it is far enough from the carriageway that leads to the manor for your chaise not to be heard by anyone within the maze walls. That way you can have your man drive right up and bring Aunt Madelaine back here without the Tonners being any the wiser. Well, what do you think? Can it be done?"

Laura was becoming more and more impressed with Elliot's plan.

"I don't see why it can't be done, as long as everything goes as you have planned it. But what shall I tell Lady Simpson-Favorite? How can I convince her to come back with me?"

Elliot thought for a moment. "I do not wish to alarm her unduly. I wonder if Uncle George has bothered to tell her that I seem to have disappeared," he mused. "No, better not to say anything about me unless she asks. You can always assure her that I am quite well and waiting for her here, though I don't know what reason you can give for that. I'm afraid you must tell her that your mother is ill. Aunt Madelaine's devotion to your mother is such that I am sure she would do anything to accommodate Lady Caroline."

"Very well," said Laura. "I shall have Martha send someone with the note at once. Then I shall have Peters or Harper drive me over in the chaise. How will you travel?"

"On foot," said Elliot, gathering up Miss Haversmith's cloak. "Give me half an hour from the time you send the note."

Laura touched Elliot's arm.

"Should anything go wrong—" she began.

Elliot refused to consider the possibility. "I can easily let myself in through the wine cellar and return to my hiding place afterward. You must come for me as soon as Aunt Madelaine arrives."

"Yes," agreed Laura. Her throat felt tight with emotion she dared not show.

They parted at the foot of the winding stairs. Laura wasted precious moments staring after Elliot. He was risking his own freedom for the sake of his aunt. How brave he was! He must succeed. Laura could not help wondering selfishly how she could hope to find Father if Elliot were caught and sent away.

She quickly turned and went in search of Martha, whom she found straightening the schoolroom. The maid took the note and promised to have it sent off at once. Before the girl left, Laura had the presence of mind to ask the whereabouts of the other members of the household.

"Miss Alexandra is playing to Miss Haversmith in the music room," said the girl. "Lady Covington is still resting in her room. We think her ladyship is worried, miss. No word from his lordship, and him gone so long," she confided, without realizing how this news would affect Laura.

Martha went off, shaking her head and leaving Laura to fight back the dreadful thoughts Martha's words inspired. She quickly squelched these with action. She went to her room to brush her hair before leaving for Lady Simpson-Favorite's.

Laura was sitting before her dressing table, idly gazing at her own reflection when she became aware that something was not right. She frowned. What could it be?

Good heavens! It was the miniature of Father. There it was in its usual place.

Laura did not know what to think. But the little likeness of her father, which had so mysteriously reappeared, made her long for him so strongly she was almost reduced to tears.

"What was it Father always said? 'Everything will come right in the end.' " Laura tried very hard to believe that.

Danger at the Manor

By the time Laura reached the stables, late afternoon mists had begun to arise. None of the stable boys seemed to be about. Laura found it necessary to call several times before Harper himself stepped outside.

"Yes, miss?" he asked. Laura noticed that his gaunt face looked more drawn than usual.

"I require the chaise, Harper," said Laura briskly. "I must go to the manor at once."

"Very good, miss," he replied, but did not respond with his accustomed alacrity. He went about the business of hitching one of Father's splendid blacks to the small carriage very slowly.

Laura did not at first take note of the singular lack of assistance, but at last she realized that Harper was quite alone.

The chaise was ready, and the coachman stood beside it waiting to assist her, when the dreadful truth struck her.

"Harper, is no one else about? Where is Peters? Where is everyone?"

"Gone, miss," replied Harper in a choked voice. "I've sent the other boys to quarters."

"Gone!" repeated Laura, her heart beating wildly with the awful knowledge that another of Elliot's predictions had come to pass. "Do you mean Peters is *gone,* Harper?"

Harper nodded.

"Oh, dear! How did it happen!"

Laura had never thought of Harper as old, for he stood quite straight and his hair had not yet begun to turn white. But today he looked old, old and tired. He shook his head in bewilderment.

"It's all so strange, miss. For two days Peters has—that is, we all have—seen a splendid white horse in the meadow. It was actually drinking, miss, from the Nailbourne itself. The poor creature had lost its rider and seemed in need of care.

"Not an hour ago Peters insisted upon going after the horse. I begged him not to, pleaded with him, I did, miss. What could a creature like that be? None of us had seen it before yesterday. It could only be a devil horse. But you know young Peters would have none of that. He has a way with animals, miss. Peters is a headstrong fellow. He went out after the horse, and he has not come back."

He rubbed the back of his hand across his eyes.

"Oh, Harper!" whispered Laura.

Did this mean that the explosion and fire Elliot had seen were about to occur? The one hope for Peters, for Giles, for Father, for all of them was Elliot!

"Harper, we have not a moment to lose," said Laura, allowing him to help her into the chaise.

The short journey to the Simpson-Favorites' was made in silence. It had been at least half an hour since the message had been sent to the Tonners. Elliot must by now be within the maze. Suppose he was unable to elude the Tonners? Suppose—But better not to think of that.

As Harper helped her down and the old butler Randolph came to greet her, Laura fervently wished it were cold enough to carry a muff to hide her trembling hands. Instead, she must be content with drawing herself up and assuming a posture of quiet dignity.

"Randolph, I've come to see Lady Simpson-Favorite with an urgent message from my mother, Lady Caroline," she said in a loud, clear voice. Randolph's deafness was a problem she had not considered. Was there anyone else about to hear her? She dared not look in the direction of the maze, which, in any case, could not be seen from here.

"Be good enough to take me to Lady Simpson-Favorite at once, Randolph."

"Oh, miss, she would be so glad to see you if she were not indisposed. Her ladyship has taken to her bed."

"I know that, Randolph. That is precisely why I have come."

Randolph hesitated a moment, then, shaking his head, he led Laura into the manor and slowly up the marble staircase.

Laura glanced neither to right nor to left for fear she would suddenly see one of the Tonners. She thought briefly of inquiring for their whereabouts, but discarded the idea. Because of Randolph's deafness, she would be obliged to speak loudly enough to arouse the entire household. No, better to hope that all had gone well and the Tonners were even now following after an impostor in a dark-blue cloak.

Randolph stood before Lady Simpson-Favorite's door and knocked. A weak voice from within bade them enter, but the butler did not hear. He was about to knock again when Laura stepped forward and motioned him aside.

"Thank you, Randolph. I'll just go on in."

She reached for the crystal knob and was astonished to find the door locked.

She looked up at Randolph.

"Why is the door locked?"

She tried again. Then Randolph tried. But the door was certainly secure.

Abandoning all caution, Laura called loudly, "Lady Simpson-Favorite, it is I, Laura Covington. Can you let us in? The door seems to be locked." She rattled the knob. "Can you unlock it? I must see you. I have a message from my mother."

There was no reply. Alarmed, Laura turned to the old butler.

"Where is the key, Randolph?" she demanded. "Surely there is a key. The housekeeper must have it. Please fetch her at once."

Randolph shook his head.

"Miss Tonner has all the keys."

"Miss Tonner!" exclaimed Laura.

By what right had Miss Tonner all the keys? Did she plan to make Lady Simpson-Favorite a prisoner in her own home?

Laura tried to think calmly.

"There must be another entrance to the room. Where is it?" she was inspired to ask and had to repeat her question, for Randolph seemed not to have understood.

"Oh, yes! Through the sitting room," he told her and led the way to that door, which blessedly was open. Laura rushed on through to the dressing room and then to Lady Simpson-Favorite's opulent bedroom.

The long windows were covered with heavy damask

draperies of crimson and gold. The gentle old lady lay upon the magnificent, canopied bed. Propped upon many pillows, she looked lost among the velvet hangings and satin quilts. Her face was very white, and her eyes were closed. She seemed to be barely breathing.

"Oh, Lady Simpson-Favorite!" exclaimed Laura.

Lady Simpson-Favorite's eyelids fluttered and then opened. She saw Laura and smiled faintly.

"So good of you to come to see me, child. Has Elliot brought you then?" she asked in a quavering voice. She reached for Laura's hand.

Laura bit her lip. How was it possible that Lady Simpson-Favorite had suddenly become so ill? Only last night she had seemed quite hearty. Elliot's suspicions must have been entirely correct.

"I'm so sorry to find you ill. Elliot hoped it was only a slight indisposition," she said.

Lady Simpson-Favorite nodded. "He is a good boy. So like his father," she said in a whisper, and her eyes closed, almost as if she might drift off to sleep.

Laura was horrified. Elliot's plan was not working at all as she had hoped. But perhaps there was still a chance to get Elliot's aunt away from the Tonners.

"Lady Simpson-Favorite," said Laura in a sharp tone. "Wouldn't you like to come along with me to the castle? Mother could make you so comfortable there. She could see to all your needs."

"Are you suggesting that I could not?"

The voice was low and heavy with indignation. Laura whirled about and nearly fainted from the shock of seeing Miss Georgina Tonner standing in the doorway.

"Well, was that your message?" demanded Miss Tonner.

Blood rushed to Laura's cheeks. She knew that in her embarrassment she must look as crimson as the bed curtains. She could think of no immediate reply and was only able to stare in awed silence. What was Miss Tonner doing here when she should have been in the maze?

"Well, was it?" Miss Tonner persisted.

"It—it was not," said Laura, finding her tongue at last. "You see, my mother was taken ill quite—quite suddenly."

Oh, dear, thought Laura. I am doing this badly. Miss Tonner won't believe a word! Nevertheless, Laura plunged ahead.

"I thought Lady Simpson-Favorite would come to her. They are close friends, you know, and Mother is so ill."

Miss Tonner's aloof expression did not change.

"Indeed!" she said. "And when you found that Lady Simpson-Favorite was ill, you thought your poor mother, in her weakened condition, could care for dear Aunt Madelaine better than I?"

Miss Tonner's eyes nearly snapped their ill will.

Laura tried to smile. "I suppose that was rather foolish of me. I—I wasn't thinking," she added weakly.

"Obviously," said Miss Tonner. "Then perhaps you will be good enough to return to your dear mother with Lady Simpson-Favorite's regrets."

She turned from Laura as though to dismiss her.

"Come, Aunt Madelaine. It is time for your medicine."

"Is it already?" Laura heard Lady Simpson-Favorite ask. "What sort of medicine is it, Georgina? It hasn't made me feel any better."

Laura left the bedroom quickly, hurried downstairs and climbed into the waiting chaise. She had Harper drive

through the gates and then stop just beyond the turn in the road.

"I'll get out here, Harper. I prefer to walk," said Laura, jumping lightly to the ground before the astonished coachman could assist her.

"But, miss—" he protested.

"Drive on, Harper," ordered Laura in her most imperious tone, and after a moment the chaise did move ahead. Laura waited until it was out of sight and then made her way back to the gates of the manor.

She must find Elliot, and the most obvious place to start was the maze. She was so upset that she could not remember the series of turns she had made earlier, nor could she remember what Elliot had said about the left wall. She rushed between the hedges blindly, trusting to luck, and soon found herself standing before the ugly statue of the satyr. She turned at the next opening to the right and was just in time to see the hem of a long, dark-colored cloak whisking around a turn ahead.

Elliot! Dare she call his name? No! She had no idea who else was in the maze. Perhaps Mr. Tonner himself. She could only follow along as swiftly as possible and hope to overtake her friend. Oh, Elliot! What had gone wrong? Laura hurried on only to find that she had somehow come back to the satyr again.

She was so disgusted by her error in judgment that she did not hear the voices nearby until it was almost too late.

"My dear Miss Haversmith, so good of you to come."

Good heavens, thought Laura. Is Miss Haversmith actually here? Have I been following her and not Elliot after all?

"Our messages must have crossed. I only just received

yours," said Mr. Tonner. "You must excuse my sister. She had duties at the house."

Laura caught her breath. So Mr. Tonner had come in answer to the forged letter and prudently had his sister remain at the house. But Miss Haversmith! What was she doing here? What did Mr. Tonner mean about messages having crossed? Had there been more than one message?

"Message? I sent no message," replied Miss Haversmith. "I came in response to your note, Mr. Tonner, and I am late because I seem to have misplaced my cloak and had to borrow another."

Laura could hardly believe the misfortune that had prompted Mr. Tonner to send for Miss Haversmith just when Elliot had formed such a clever plan. Now everything was ruined. Mr. Tonner would discover both Elliot and herself.

"You sent no message, and your cloak was missing?" asked Mr. Tonner. He had obviously been taken in and was now confused. Perhaps there was still time to find Elliot.

"I wonder—" began Mr. Tonner and then broke off.

"However," Miss Haversmith said, "I was pleased to receive your message to meet here, because I believe I do have information that will interest you."

"What sort of information do you have?" asked Mr. Tonner eagerly.

Miss Haversmith spoke quickly, and her voice was low. Laura had to strain to hear.

"The boy is most certainly hiding in Covington Castle. Cook prepared a second tea tray for Laura after the child had had an ample tea of her own. I suspect she carried the tray to some hiding place."

"Now that explains a good deal," said Mr. Tonner. "It is good news. I thank you for it. It should not be difficult for us to find Elliot. You, my dear, can certainly outwit poor, misguided little Laura. She probably has no idea how dangerous my nephew is. I daresay he is safe for the moment. I have a more pressing problem. It concerns Sir Edward."

Laura stood rigid and alert at the sound of her father's name.

"Have you any idea of his exact whereabouts?"

"Was he not in London?" the governess asked. "I am sure her ladyship sent to London to fetch him home when the trouble became worse in the village."

"According to my sources," said Mr. Tonner, "Sir Edward could not have gone to London. In fact he was seen in Dover only two days ago. Thanks to your cleverness in obtaining that small picture of his lordship, my man was able to identify him."

Laura's indignation at learning that it was Miss Haversmith who had taken her miniature was fortunately overcome by her desire to learn more of her father. Her first impulse was to step around the hedge and confront her governess, but she repressed it.

"Dover! Why should Sir Edward go to Dover when he said he was going to London? I am sure he said he was going to London. I am sure of it."

"My dear," said Mr. Tonner, "a small falsehood like that does not surprise me. Smuggling is a dirty business."

"Smuggling!" cried Miss Haversmith.

"Yes, smuggling. I am afraid it is the business of smuggling that occupies Sir Edward."

"No!" Miss Haversmith sounded as horrified as Laura felt.

"I am only sorry that you, my dear, must be connected with such an infamous household. This is a misfortune I hope I shall have the happiness to correct very soon."

"Oh, Mr. Tonner!" Miss Haversmith's usual cool tones were full of emotion.

Laura did not know what foolish move she might have made if she had not been startled by the shrill sound of some kind of whistle. She had the uncanny sensation that she had heard the sound before, but could not think where.

"I am afraid I have detained you too long, Miss Haversmith," said Mr. Tonner. "Allow me to escort you to your chaise."

"I did not come in the chaise, thank you, sir. I was on foot."

"Surely I saw the Covington chaise draw up," replied Mr. Tonner.

"That may very well be," said Miss Haversmith, "but it was not I who rode in it."

"How very curious!" said Mr. Tonner. "Here we turn to the left."

Laura froze. They were surely coming this way. She looked frantically about and saw the statue of the satyr. Even as she gazed upon the fiendish image, the creature moved and spoke her name. Was it calling her? Beckoning her? Was it a devil sent by the evil waters to lure her away?

Terrified, Laura sank to the ground in a faint.

The Hidden Sloop

Satyr. Satan. Devil. Devil Waters. The Nailbourne! Laura fought her way back to consciousness, certain she had been taken.

At first she thought Miss Haversmith was bending over her as she lay in the damp grass. But it was only Elliot in Miss Haversmith's cloak. He was rubbing her wrists vigorously.

"Laura! Laura! Do open your eyes! Come round, please. I never meant this to happen."

Laura not only opened her eyes, she struggled to get up.

"Quickly, Elliot! We must leave this place at once. They mean to take me. The Devil Waters! Elliot," she cried, grasping his hand, "the satyr moved."

"Yes," said Elliot calmly. "It was I who moved him. Look!"

He went to the statue, which leered down upon them with an ugly stare. Elliot pushed at the white marble legs with all his might. Slowly the statue swung away from its pedestal, revealing a flight of stone stairs that led into darkness below.

"I'm sorry I frightened you," said Elliot, "but we had to hide or we would have been discovered. I called to you to join me on these stairs, but you fainted. I didn't blame you, of course. You must have been awfully frightened. I can imagine what you must have thought. Well, I had to drag you inside to wait until Uncle George and Miss Haversmith had gone. I brought you out as soon as it was safe."

"Good heavens! Where do those stairs lead?" asked Laura. She hated to think that she had been on those dark, mysterious steps at all. They were damp and probably covered with cobwebs.

"I don't know, and it is too dark to investigate. I'm only thankful that when I came upon the satyr earlier, it was slightly off center, or I would never have discovered such a convenient hiding place."

Elliot sighed and shook his head regretfully. "I'm afraid I've made a muddle of everything. Were you able to see Aunt Madelaine at all? I suppose it was impossible to get her away from Aunt Georgina."

"I'm afraid so," said Laura. "But you must not blame yourself. We had to do something. And, Elliot, you were right about Lady Simpson-Favorite. Something is very wrong there. She is kept locked in her rooms and Miss Tonner has the keys."

As they made their way slowly out of the maze, Laura launched into a description of her visit, including every detail of the conversation with Miss Tonner.

"I think the time has come to tell your mother everything," said Elliot. "She is the only one who can help Aunt Madelaine. You shall have to do it. I dare not return with you now. Aunt Madelaine might need me. I shall keep out of sight as long as I possibly can. But I cannot do this indefinitely. You must get help to us."

"Of course, Elliot. But what of Father? Why is Mr. Tonner so interested in him? And why should Father go to Dover secretly?"

"Have you never heard it mentioned that your father might be a voluntary member of the King's revenue men?"

"You mean the men who investigate smugglers? Father? I hardly think so, Elliot."

"Why not?" asked Elliot. "Dover is one of the most important southern ports. It is nearby. It is well known that despite the law against trading with France during these difficult years of Napoleon's reign, brandy and wines find their way into inns and homes. Many dishonest people will buy from smugglers. Smuggling is more profitable than ever. A man like your father, who is loyal to the King, might do all in his power to fight these wicked people."

"Then you think Mr. Tonner is a smuggler!"

"I would not be surprised," said Elliot.

"Do you think Father knows about—" began Laura, but stopped because Elliot stood staring ahead at nothing she could see. The look of surprise and horror on his face was dreadful to behold.

"The spire," whispered Elliot hoarsely.

Laura spoke not a word. He seemed not to be aware of her. He was looking at something beyond this time and place. She must not distract him. Perhaps this time he would see more.

"The men! The men!" cried Elliot. "How pitiful!"

Laura watched him fascinated. What did he see?

Elliot closed his eyes and then opened them again, but it was obvious that the yew hedge had become only a hedge again. Whatever he had been seeing had vanished.

He turned to Laura, his eyes blazing with understanding.

"It was not a spire at all. It was so high and straight. I thought it must be a spire, but it is not."

"What is it?" demanded Laura. "Tell me."

"It's a mast. A ship's mast! There is a ship in the hidden cove, and your father is aboard her. I must warn him at once."

Elliot broke into a run with Laura close behind him. They raced across the manor lawns toward the stables. Once they had left the maze, Laura could not keep up with him, though she tried. He was already saddling his own horse, much to the astonishment of the stable boys, when Laura reached him.

"You must not come, Laura," said Elliot. "There could be an explosion at any moment."

Laura did not bother to argue, nor did she wait for a saddle. Grasping the mane of the nearest horse, she pulled herself up and, in most unladylike fashion, sat astride as Elliot did, tearing her skirt as she moved. What did that matter? Father was in danger.

Though she had never heard of a ship coming into the cove, because of the shallowness of the water, she had implicit faith in Elliot and never doubted him for a moment.

"Stay back, Laura," ordered Elliot once more, as he rode off.

"I must go to Father," insisted Laura, as they both streaked past the amazed stable boys, making straight for the manor gates.

They had just passed through the gates when two men sprang up as if from nowhere and accosted Elliot, snatching the reins from his hands and dragging him from his horse.

"Get away, Laura," shouted Elliot before one of them knocked him unconscious.

Laura stifled a cry. She pulled her horse about. For a moment it seemed that the spirited animal might throw her. He reared on his hind legs, and his forelegs pawed the air wildly.

Laura clung desperately to the thick mane. After a moment the frightened animal recovered himself. She urged him back past the maze and the rear gardens, where she soon found the low hedge she and Elliot had jumped that morning. What would become of Elliot, she did not know. She felt she must find Father and warn him. Father would know what to do about Elliot. Father would make everything right again.

Laura crossed the main road and gained the grove of elm trees that banked the southern boundary of the common meadow. Instinctively she kept to these, for they covered her approach. It was evening, and the sun cast long shadows, making it easier to hide. She wondered if there were men set to guard the area. Surely the entry of a ship into the cove was secret. If it had anything to do with smugglers, the crew would not welcome visitors. But she saw no one.

Laura looked toward the willows that hid the cove. Yes, there above the trees, higher still than the arms of the old windmill, was a mast. But one had almost to know that it was there to see it, for it was so well hidden.

Laura slowed the horse to a complete standstill, wondering how best to approach the ship and where she might find Father. Was he aboard even now, or was that something that was only about to happen?

Laura knew she could afford to wait no longer. She would have to make a dash for it. Best to leave the horse

behind. A runner on foot would be far less conspicuous. Laura slid to the ground, speaking soft words of praise to her horse and bidding him to stay behind.

The mist and haze of early evening had begun to hide the sun. Perhaps if she stayed beside the trees until the very last moment, she would not be seen. Whatever the risk, she had to take it. As far as Laura could see, there was not a soul about. Softly she crept to the last of the elms and then, gathering all her strength, she ran across the narrowest part of the open meadow and hid herself behind a screen of willow branches.

As she ran, she sighted the waters of the Nailbourne. They seemed broader and fuller than ever as they flowed toward the cove. Naturally they would have raised the level of the water sufficiently to allow the entrance of a ship, she realized with sudden insight. How convenient for smugglers not to have to chance coming into one of the main ports like Dover!

Safely behind the willows, Laura looked up. The black hull of the sloop rose so unexpectedly before her that it struck terror in her heart. But she did not cry out. There was not a sound in the cove, not even the usual twittering of birds as they roosted for the night. All was silent as death itself. Beside the cove stood the crumbling windmill. Had that been used as a smugglers' hiding place?

Frightened as she was, Laura felt she must board the ship and look for her father. But she could see no way to do this. The sails were furled. The ship rode at anchor, and yet she saw no sign of a gangplank. How did one approach the ship?

Ever careful to keep the screen of willow branches between herself and the ship, Laura moved toward the starboard side, nearest the windmill.

There was her answer! A crude, makeshift jetty had been constructed, leading from the mill to a rope ladder. Without a thought for her own safety, Laura stole across the jetty, tucked up her skirts, and climbed aboard.

As she reached the deck, she peered cautiously about. No one was in sight. She was just wondering what to do next, when she heard voices behind her.

Laura dropped down and inched her way toward a huge coil of rope that would hide her from view. In the midst of her danger, the bizarre thought crossed her mind that Miss Haversmith or Mother should see her now.

In her terror she soon forgot both her governess and her mother, for she heard Mr. Tonner's voice.

"Ahoy, Captain! We have another victim of the Nailbourne for you. He's young and scrawny, but should make a cabin boy. Captain!" he shouted loudly. "Where the devil is he?"

For a moment, Laura thought Mr. Tonner was alone and wondered whom he meant by another victim of the Nailbourne. But seconds later his companion's head appeared over the side. The man glared about angrily.

"In his cups again, I'll warrant. I told you not to hire Walters, Tonner. I warned you," grumbled the man. "But, no, you had to have that old rumpot for your captain. There were other men of experience you might have chosen."

"Ah, yes, but not men of his cunning, Carstairs. You seem to forget. We deal in danger and devilry. Captain Walters is used to both," replied Mr. Tonner coldly. "You also seem to forget that I am in charge here. We agreed on that. You may be the proprietor of Black Swan Inn, but I am in charge here. I make the decisions. Anytime you don't like the arrangement, you can tell me, and I shall take my brandy elsewhere. There are plenty who will pay the price."

The threat obviously worried Carstairs. He answered in a much subdued tone, "Don't be so touchy. It was only meant as a suggestion."

Laura watched with horror as he clambered aboard with Elliot's unconscious body slung unceremoniously over his shoulder.

Laura had seen Mr. Carstairs only a few times before when she had ridden past the Inn on the way to Tonbridge Wells, but she recognized him. He was a heavyset man with light hair and a wide, jowly face. So he was Mr. Tonner's partner! They were both smugglers as Elliot had guessed. Poor, poor Elliot! He looked so still and limp.

"It may be," said Carstairs, "that the blow I gave him was uncommonly hard for such a slip of a fellow. You sure he's not dead?"

Laura bit her lip and clenched her hands until her nails dug into her palms. Elliot couldn't, he must not, be dead!

She watched Carstairs lay him down on the deck, while Mr. Tonner felt about for a pulse and then grunted with satisfaction.

"You're an alarmist, Carstairs. He's alive. He has as hard a head as his father. Remember the time we captured him?" Mr. Tonner laughed unpleasantly. "And whose fault was it that he got away that time, eh, Carstairs? Would you like to remember that?"

"I couldn't watch him every minute," protested the unhappy Carstairs. "So he got away. So what! He wouldn't tell on his own half brother. By the time we were through, why, it looked as though he were to blame for the smuggling. And who would have believed him then? It didn't hurt us any."

126

"Didn't it?" asked Mr. Tonner. "We had to leave the cove in a hurry. We had to give up the sport of kidnapping men from Tonbridge Wells without anyone suspecting it was us instead of their devil waters. We had to use the larger ports to dock. We were almost caught, you fool! And you say it didn't hurt!"

"Do you have to remember every mistake, Tonner?" Carstairs shook his head in disgust. "Forgive and forget. Nobody's perfect."

For a moment the two men stood glaring at each other. Finally Mr. Tonner shrugged.

"This is no time to quarrel. We're partners, and we've done well up to now. Here, I'll put the boy with the others. You rouse the captain. As soon as the crew gets back, we should start out."

Carstairs grunted and made his way toward the cabin in the prow of the ship. Mr. Tonner bound Elliot's hands with a length of rope, then carried him toward the hold.

When he disappeared below, Laura tried to relax and breathe deeply. She suddenly realized she had been breathing hardly at all these past few minutes for fear of being discovered. She wished she could stand and stretch her cramped, aching legs, but dared not give herself away.

After a few moments Carstairs stuck his head out of the cabin door.

"Tonner!" he shouted. "You'd better come here and help me. I told you the old boy had been drinking again."

"Don't lose your head!" snapped Mr. Tonner, reappearing on deck. "He'll come round. He always does."

He and Carstairs disappeared inside the captain's cabin.

Laura lost no time in scrambling across the deck to the gangway down which Mr. Tonner had carried Elliot. She descended the narrow ladder blindly. It was not yet possible to see in the dim light from the open hatch, but she was instantly aware that she was not alone. She was completely surrounded by living, breathing human beings. Although she could not see them in the darkness, she knew they were there. Were they friends or enemies?

Then, softly, somewhere near her feet, she heard a low moaning.

"Elliot! Elliot!" she whispered.

Laura knelt and worked loose the rope that held his hands.

"Elliot, can you hear me?"

There was no reply.

Frightened, Laura touched his face and felt the blood oozing from the cut on the side of his head.

The Explosion

"Miss Laura! Can it be?" came a hoarse whisper.

Elliot moaned and stirred again at her feet. Laura tried hard to see who had spoken. She thought the voice was familiar, but she could not be sure.

"Who is it?" she asked fearfully.

"Giles, miss. Ye haven't forgotten me?"

"Giles! Oh, Giles! I thought you were—" Laura broke off. "Giles, what are you doing here?"

"We all be here, miss. Peters, Robert Bombray, and all the others they could get their bloody hands on, the scum!"

Gradually Laura was able to perceive Giles's pitiful form. His hands were manacled, and he wore leg-irons as well. So did all the other men who sat helplessly staring up at her.

"But why? What is the meaning of this?" demanded Laura.

"They mean to sell us to the French, or even the Spanish. They don't care which," Peters informed her. "They be desperate, evil men. It ain't the Nailbourne or the mists

129

that be evil. It be the men. They tell the story of the waters at the tavern in the Inn so that no one will go out on the meadow near the cove and find the ship.

"It all be the evil doing of the men. Smugglers is what they are. They be smuggling French brandy in and good men out."

Laura had once heard her father say that the enemies of England paid highly for men to man their ships. And they didn't care how they got the men so long as they were strong and healthy.

"They took me first," said Giles. "Ye saw it, miss. They'd not be expecting his lordship in the meadow. I heard them say it. Ye near saved me, your friend did. They near give up. But then the mists come so sudden and hid what they did. It be their chance to knock me unconscious and take me off without your seeing. Here I was in chains before I knew it."

"Why, that's—that's monstrous," cried Laura. She reached out and grasped the heavy chains that held Giles. "How can I free you?"

"Behind ye, miss, are the keys. They be hanging in plain sight so to torture us," replied Giles.

"I'll get them at once," said Laura. Her eyes had grown used to the dark now, and she turned and saw the key ring hanging above her. She stretched as far as she could. The keys were just out of reach.

"I'm not tall enough," she wailed and looked about for something to stand on. There was nothing.

Elliot had regained consciousness and was sitting up now. He gingerly touched his bloody wound.

"What happened? Where am I? Laura? Is that you?"

Laura fell to her knees, reached beneath her long skirt

and ripped off a length of her petticoat. This she pressed gently to Elliot's forehead.

"Don't bother about me," said Elliot. "Can we be on the ship? You must get off at once."

"I will! I will! We all will!" promised Laura. "First we must release the men. They are manacled and the keys are out of my reach. We must hurry before Mr. Tonner returns."

Elliot understood the situation at once. He crawled painfully to the wall.

"Climb on my back," he ordered. "Quickly!"

Laura did as she was told and succeeded in obtaining the keys. In seconds Giles was free and had begun to release the others.

"If this is the ship, where is the crew? Where is the captain?" asked Elliot.

"Gone to deliver the casks of brandy they been smuggling," said Peters. "They be carrying eighty casks. I heard them say it. Some were for the Black Swan Inn and delivered yesterday. The men be out hiding the rest somewhere hereabouts."

"The captain's had too much to drink," added Laura and told what she had overheard. "They must be trying to sober him."

"But your father," said Elliot, getting unsteadily to his feet. "Have none of you men seen or heard Lord Covington on board?"

There were murmurs of surprise and denial. No one had seen him.

"He's here! I know he is," said Elliot. "We must find him. And you must leave the ship at once, Laura."

"Not without you and Father," said Laura stubbornly.

"There is no time to argue," snapped Elliot. "You must do as I say."

The freed men had risen to their feet and were rubbing their arms and legs.

"Beggin' your pardon, sir," said Giles. "It be best if we climb up before the crew comes. We can take care of the captain now."

"And Tonner and Carstairs," added Peters.

"Right you are, Giles," said Elliot. "And the moment we are on deck, Laura, you must get off."

Laura sighed and said nothing. Giles led the way. Quiet as cats, the men followed. Once on deck they kept low and advanced toward the cabin. Elliot pushed Laura toward the rail and would have forced her overboard if the door of the captain's cabin had not suddenly been thrown open, and Carstairs, Mr. Tonner, and the captain burst out. Laura and Elliot hid themselves, as did the others.

The captain was still obviously far from sober. He swayed and stumbled after the other two, swinging a small, lighted lantern and mumbling to himself. He was certainly the most disreputable-looking sea captain Laura had ever seen. His cap was pulled low over his eyes, and his whiskers were ragged and matted.

"What is keeping the crew?" demanded Mr. Tonner impatiently. "Now that we've got this wretch on his feet, we might get under way. We'll never be able to make contact with the French frigate once the fog sets in and gets thicker. I want to be rid of those boys tonight," he added, nodding toward the open hatch. "We must start. Pipe the signal, Carstairs, will you? How long does it take the crew to hide the casks beneath the statue in the maze?"

Elliot and Laura exchanged a look of understanding.

The mysterious steps must have led to a cache of smuggled brandy, and the horrible, grinning statue of the satyr held the secret fast.

"That all depends," retorted Carstairs, "on how many casks of brandy the men have opened. One of us should have stayed behind to watch them."

"I rather thought that capturing my nephew was a bit more important at the time," said Mr. Tonner dryly. "He knows too much. Heaven only knows where the girl went or what sort of mischief she is up to. Pipe the signal."

Laura realized Mr. Tonner was speaking of her. She shrank back behind the coil of rope.

The sound Carstairs made with the ship's pipe was sharp and pierced the air shrilly. Laura remembered that she had heard it before. Once in the maze this evening and also last night when she had been awakened by Miss Haversmith as she took the miniature. This sloop, she decided, must have been coming in and out of the cove for some time, for as long as the men of Tonbridge Wells had been disappearing while the people blamed the tragedies on the Nailbourne. What horrible creatures these smugglers were! But where was Father? Had they taken him to sell to some French frigate captain, too? A feeling of hopelessness had begun to settle upon Laura. Perhaps Elliot had misunderstood his vision, and Father was not here at all.

In the distance, now, Laura could hear the crew approaching. Some of them were singing, and as they came closer, it was obvious all of them had been drinking.

From the corner of her eye Laura saw Elliot and Giles exchange a signal. Led by Giles, the men leaped from their hiding places and beset the astonished Carstairs and Mr.

Tonner. The angry men would have taken the captain, too, but the stooped figure straightened suddenly and threw off his cap and false whiskers.

"Edward!" The name seemed to be torn from Mr. Tonner. "No, it can't be!"

"Father!" cried Laura. "Oh, Father!" And she ran to his arms.

Lord Covington set down the small lantern and held his daughter tightly, lifting her right off the deck.

"Laura! Good heavens! What are you doing here? And Elliot too!"

He looked past Laura at Mr. Tonner.

"Well, George, it's been a long time."

George Tonner's small eyes narrowed, and his mouth twisted with anger. "Not long enough," he said.

"More than twelve years," said Lord Covington, placing Laura down on the deck. She stood beside him clinging to his hand.

"I confess I did not expect you, Edward," said Tonner. "I had it on the best authority that you were in Dover. You were seen there."

"Yes, but I've come back. I've been following your activities quite closely, George. The revenue men wondered why you had moved north. Then I saw the Nailbourne and knew you were using the cove again. Naturally I rode into Dover and told them."

"You've been spying on us," said Mr. Tonner. "The white horse—I suppose that was yours."

Father smiled calmly. "You saw him then? I meant to worry you, George, so I bought him in Dover. He's very like Darley, the one your half brother used to ride, isn't he?"

"I don't believe in ghosts," said Mr. Tonner disdainfully.

"Perhaps you should, George." Laura's father shook his head. His smile was gone. "I've been haunted by the desire to capture you all these years. Do you realize what you did to Elliot by casting the suspicion of smuggling on him? He was never able to return to Tonbridge Wells. It was the greatest disappointment of his life. Did you know that?"

"He was a fool. We could have made him rich. But, no, he was too good for us," growled Carstairs, but Mr. Tonner said nothing.

"You are quite right, sir. He was just that. Much too good for you," said Lord Covington proudly. "He was the finest man I ever knew."

He sighed then and shrugged. "Well, it's over now. We shall clear your father's name, shan't we, young Elliot?" he asked.

"Oh, sir," cried Elliot. "I do thank you from the bottom of my heart. I am most grateful. But we must leave this ship at once. It is doomed."

As Elliot spoke, the voices of the approaching crew made it apparent that they were about to board the ship.

"Yes," agreed Lord Covington, "it is doomed to end its dastardly career. Lads," he said, looking at the men of Tonbridge Wells, "I meant to free you and capture the lot of them once we were under way. Let us do it now. Let the crew come aboard, and then we'll take them. Laura, you and Elliot get back. Stay out of the way."

The men dragged the defeated Mr. Tonner and Carstairs out of sight and hid themselves.

Elliot was about to protest, but stopped when he saw

the first crewman appear at the rail. The other men followed, clambering clumsily aboard. Lord Covington, having replaced his cap and whiskers, resumed his stooped posture and watched them come. With the last man aboard, he gave the order to weigh anchor. Soon the men were hauling ropes. Yards and yards of canvas were hoisted up the mainsail.

At first no one saw the strange figure in white knitted underwear stumble from the captain's cabin. But they heard the pistol shot. A stooped man with wild hair and ragged whiskers had fired into the air. He swayed as he spoke, much the worse for the bottle of French brandy he had drunk.

Laura realized at once that this was the real captain. Father must have taken the man's clothes in order to disguise himself.

"Avast there, the scurvy lot of ya. Who gave the order to weigh anchor? Is it mutiny then?" roared the furious captain.

The crew gazed in astonishment from Lord Covington to the real captain.

"Shoot him, Walters, shoot!" shouted Mr. Tonner, who was instantly knocked unconscious by Giles. When Carstairs tried to break away, he received the same treatment.

Captain Walters advanced on Lord Covington, a pistol in each hand. "Steal me ship! Strip me of me clothes and push me into a sea chest, will ye?" he said.

Waving his pistols menacingly, he tried to stride forward and stumbled into the lighted lantern that Lord Covington had set on the deck.

At once a coil of rope caught fire. Small flames licked at it hungrily and grew as they found old rags and rotted wood to feed upon. The fire moved relentlessly toward a barrel plainly marked in large black letters, GUN POW-DER.

"Abandon ship! Men, jump!" shouted Lord Covington.

The captain and crew were too befuddled by drink to respond in time. But Father turned and scooped up Laura with one arm. He and Elliot joined the men of Tonbridge Wells at the rail and they all plunged into the murky, black waters of the cove.

Laura gasped and spluttered. Water filled her mouth and nostrils. But Father still held her tightly about the waist, and she was not afraid.

Only Father and Elliot seemed to know anything at all about swimming. The other men splashed and kicked wildly in an effort to get clear of the sloop. They managed to keep afloat somehow, grasping pieces of broken barrels that had toppled overboard with them.

Laura chanced to look back just as the flames must have reached the gunpowder. The explosion was deafening. Red, orange, and yellow flames leaped up and out. The sloop appeared to break in two. Pieces of burning wood flew through the air in all directions. No one aboard would have survived.

"Poor devils," whispered Father.

Yes, poor devils, thought Laura. But if it had not been for Elliot, would not Father and all the other men have been killed? She wondered how Elliot felt about his strange gift now. He had released and saved at least a score of men who might have been burned to death.

"I think it's gone," said Elliot.

"Gone!" echoed Laura. "What makes you think so?"

They had climbed the old tree in the walled garden and were just settling down for a pleasant chat, while the

137

adults and Alexandra enjoyed tea on the terrace.

Lady Simpson-Favorite had made a remarkable recovery the moment Miss Tonner had left her household and stopped giving Elliot's old aunt the unusual medicine.

"Well," said Elliot, "it's been two weeks and there's been no sign of anything. I haven't seen a thing out of the ordinary."

He sounded rather pleased. Laura did not like to discourage him, but she felt she must point out that perhaps there had not been anything for him to see.

"No necessity, so to speak," she said.

Elliot sighed. "Perhaps," he said. "Still, it would be such a relief."

Laura looked off toward the common meadow where the cows and sheep were grazing contentedly once more. Some of them quenched their thirst with the waters of the Nailbourne. Now that the villagers understood and believed the true source of the waters, they thought it convenient to have the stream in the meadow. Father said it could not last, though. Its waters were already dwindling. Soon it would disappear as mysteriously as it had come.

"I wonder if we shall ever see Miss Haversmith again," mused Laura.

Miss Haversmith had confessed her shameful behavior to Lord and Lady Covington. It seemed that she had developed a secret attachment for Mr. Tonner years ago when she had first come to Covington Castle.

"Mr. Tonner convinced me then that it was he who was with the King's men. Later I even believed that it was Lord Covington who was engaged in smuggling. Of course I shall resign my position at once," she said.

Although Laura's father and mother professed to understand and forgive her, Miss Haversmith insisted upon

138

leaving. She was too ashamed to stay on.

"It is too bad she had to go," said Laura. "I was just beginning to like her, a little, anyway. She wasn't all that bad, do you think?"

She turned to look at Elliot, but he was not listening. He was staring in that familiar way straight ahead at nothing she could see. For a moment Laura was frightened. Then she noticed that Elliot's pleasant expression had not changed. He was actually smiling.

"I think Miss Haversmith will be happy enough. She's going to be married."

"Why, Elliot! How wonderful for her!"

"And for me, too," said Elliot. "Do you realize that is the first time I've seen something other than a disaster?"

Laura laughed aloud. "Elliot! I knew it. You *can* turn an evil gift to good, after all!"